T0214639

Lecture Notes in Computer Science 11264

Commenced Publication in 1973
Founding and Former Series Editors:
Gerhard Goos, Juris Hartmanis, and Jan van Leeuwen

More information about this series at http://www.springer.com/series/7412

Xiang Bai · Yi Fang · Yangqing Jia ·
Meina Kan · Shiguang Shan ·
Chunhua Shen · Jingdong Wang ·
Gui-Song Xia · Shuicheng Yan ·
Zhaoxiang Zhang · Kamal Nasrollahi ·
Gang Hua · Thomas B. Moeslund ·
Qiang Ji (Eds.)

Video Analytics

Face and Facial Expression Recognition

Third International Workshop, FFER 2018
and Second International Workshop, DLPR 2018
Beijing, China, August 20, 2018
Revised Selected Papers

 Springer

Editors
Xiang Bai
Huazhong University of Science and
Technology
Wuhan, China

Yi Fang
New York University Abu Dhabi
Abu Dhabi, UAE

Yangqing Jia
Facebook (United States)
San Francisco, CA, USA

Meina Kan
Chinese Academy of Sciences
Beijing, China

Shiguang Shan
Chinese Academy of Sciences
Beijing, China

Chunhua Shen
University of Adelaide
Adeladie, SA, Australia

Jingdong Wang
Microsoft Research Asia (China)
Beijing, China

Gui-Song Xia
Wuhan University
Wuhan, China

Shuicheng Yan
National University of Singapore
Singapore, Singapore

Zhaoxiang Zhang
Chinese Academy of Sciences
Beijing, China

Kamal Nasrollahi
Aalborg University
Aalborg, Denmark

Gang Hua
Microsoft Research
Seattle, WA, USA

Thomas B. Moeslund
Aalborg University
Aalborg, Denmark

Qiang Ji
Rensselaer Polytechnic Institute
Troy, NY, USA

ISSN 0302-9743   ISSN 1611-3349   (electronic)
Lecture Notes in Computer Science
ISBN 978-3-030-12176-1   ISBN 978-3-030-12177-8   (eBook)
https://doi.org/10.1007/978-3-030-12177-8

Library of Congress Control Number: 2018968328

LNCS Sublibrary: SL6 – Image Processing, Computer Vision, Pattern Recognition, and Graphics

This Springer imprint is published by the registered company Springer Nature Switzerland AG
The registered company address is: Gewerbestrasse 11, 6330 Cham, Switzerland

Preface

The DLPR workshop was formerly known as the International Workshop on Deep Learning for Pattern Recognition. This workshop was first held in conjunction with the 23rd International Conference on Pattern Recognition (ICPR 2016). The second workshop was held in conjunction with ICPR 2018, and was jointly organized with the Workshop on Face and Facial Expression Recognition from Real World Videos (FFER). The purpose of this workshop is to bring together researchers who are working on developing deep learning and pattern recognition to report or exchange their progress in deep learning for pattern recognition. The reviewing was single-blind, and about 20 external expert reviewers from the community were invited to help with specific papers. Each paper was reviewed by at least three reviewers. To come to a final consensus on the papers for the program and these proceedings, an online meeting was held where each paper was discussed. Finally, the committee selected seven papers from nine submissions, covering various topics in pattern recognition including histopathological images, action recognition, scene text detection, speech recognition, object classification, presentation attack detection, and driver drowsiness detection. All papers were presented as oral papers. Moreover, there were two invited keynotes and more than 40 researchers attended this workshop.

We would like to express our gratitude to all our colleagues for submitting papers to the DLPR and FFER workshops, and all the reviewers for their contribution.

January 2019

Xiang Bai
Yi Fang
Yangqing Jia
Meina Kan
Shiguang Shan
Chunhua Shen
Jingdong Wang
Gui-Song Xia
Shuicheng Yan
Zhaoxiang Zhang
Kamal Nasrollahi
Gang Hua
Thomas B. Moeslund
Qiang Ji

Organization

DLPR Organizers

Xiang Bai — Huazhong University of Science and Technology, Wuhan, China
Yi Fang — New York University Abu Dhabi and New York University, Abu Dhabi, UAE
Yangqing Jia — Facebook, San Francisco, USA
Meina Kan — ICT, Chinese Academy of Sciences, Beijing, China
Shiguang Shan — ICT, Chinese Academy of Sciences, Beijing, China
Chunhua Shen — University of Adelaide, Australia
Jingdong Wang — Microsoft Research Asia, Beijing, China
Gui-Song Xia — Wuhan University, China
Shuicheng Yan — National University of Singapore, Singapore
Zhaoxiang Zhang — Institute of Automation, Chinese Academy of Sciences, Beijing, China

FFER Organizers

Kamal Nasrollahi — Aalborg University, Denmark
Gang Hua — Microsoft Research, Seattle, USA
Thomas B. Moeslund — Aalborg University, Denmark
Qiang Ji — Rensselaer Polytechnic Institute, USA

Reviewers

Albert Ali Salah — Bogazici University, Turkey
Anastasios Doulamis — Technical University of Crete, Greece
Andrea Lagorio — University of Sassari, Italy
François Brémond — Inria Sophia Antipolis, France
Gholamreza Anbarjafari — University of Tartu, Estonia
Gian Luca Foresti — University of Udine, Italy
Gonzàlez Jordi — Universitat Autònoma de Barcelona, Spain
Greg Mori — Simon Fraser University, Canada
Hans-Albert Löbel Díaz — Catholic University of Chile, Chile
Hedvig Kjellström — KTH Royal Institute of Technology, Sweden
Hugo Jair Escalante — INAOE, Mexico
Jeffrey Cohn — University of Pittsburgh, USA
Jianxin Wu — Nanjing University, China
Jose Alba-Castro — Vigo University, Spain
Lijun Yin — State University of New York at Binghamton, USA
Massimo Tistarelli — University of Sassari, Italy

Contents

Convolutional Neural Network-Based Classification of Histopathological Images Affected by Data Imbalance

Michał Koziarski[✉], Bogdan Kwolek, and Bogusław Cyganek

Department of Electronics, AGH University of Science and Technology,
Al. Mickiewicza 30, 30-059 Kraków, Poland
michal.koziarski@agh.edu.pl

Abstract. In this paper we experimentally evaluated the impact of data imbalance on the convolutional neural networks performance in the histopathological image recognition task. We conducted our analysis on the Breast Cancer Histopathological Database. We considered four phenomena associated with data imbalance: how does it affect classification performance, what strategies of preventing imbalance are suitable for histopathological data, how presence of imbalance affects the value of new observations, and whether sampling training data from a balanced distribution during data acquisition is beneficial if test data will remain imbalanced. The most important findings of our experimental analysis are the following: while high imbalance significantly affects the performance, for some of the metrics small imbalance. Sampling training data from a balanced distribution had a decremental effect, and we achieved a better performance applying a dedicated strategy of dealing with imbalance. Finally, not all of the traditional strategies of dealing with imbalance translate well to the histopathological image recognition setting.

Keywords: Convolutional neural network · Data imbalance · Histopathological image classification

1 Introduction

Due to the recent algorithmic advances, as well as a growing amount of data and computational resources, machine learning is becoming increasingly suitable option for the task of histopathological data processing. In particular, deep learning methods are becoming dominant technique in the field [4]. A significant amount of work has been done by the scientific community on the problem of using deep learning algorithms in the histopathological image recognition task. However, despite that, a little attention has been given to the issue of data imbalance in the histopathological setting, or more generally in the image recognition task. Data imbalance [9] can be defined as a situation, in which the number of observations from one of the classes (majority class) is higher than the number

© Springer Nature Switzerland AG 2019
X. Bai et al. (Eds.): FFER 2018/DLPR 2018, LNCS 11264, pp. 1–11, 2019.
https://doi.org/10.1007/978-3-030-12177-8_1

of observations from another class (minority class). Most of the existing machine learning algorithms assume a balanced data distribution, and perform poorly in an imbalanced setting, biasing predictions towards the majority class. Notably, data imbalance can be observed in various existing histopathological benchmark datasets, such as Breast Cancer Histopathological Database (BreakHis) [14]. It is, however, unclear to what extent data imbalance affects the performance of deep learning algorithms in the histopathological image recognition task, or what techniques of dealing with data imbalance are suitable in such setting. In a recent study Pulgar et al. [12] evaluate the impact of data imbalance on the performance of convolutional neural networks in the traffic sign recognition task. They conclude that data imbalance negatively affects the performance of neural networks. They do not, however, consider using any strategies of dealing with data imbalance. In another study by Buda et al. [1] the authors also evaluate the impact of data imbalance on the performance of convolutional neural networks, this time evaluating some of the existing strategies of dealing with imbalance. However, neither of the mentioned papers uses the histopathological data. Furthermore, in this study we consider additional questions related to the issue of data imbalance, namely the value of new observations in the imbalanced data setting and the choice of strategy of dealing with imbalance. Finally, it is worth mentioning a study by Lusa [11], in which the author experimentally evaluates the performance of one of the most prevalent strategies of dealing with data imbalance, SMOTE [2], on a high-dimensional data. Based on that study, SMOTE is not suitable for dealing with a high-dimensional data, such as images. It is not clear whether other strategies of dealing with imbalance translate well into the histopathological image setting.

In this paper we extend on the previous research, in particular focusing on the problem of histopathological image recognition. We experimentally evaluate various trends associated with data imbalance. First of all, we test to what extent data imbalance influences the classification performance. Secondly, we evaluate various strategies of dealing with data imbalance. Thirdly, we measure how data imbalance influences the value of new data. Finally, we test the hypothesis that artificially balancing the training distribution during data can be beneficial for performance, even if the test distribution is imbalanced.

2   Experimental Study

2.1   Set-Up

Dataset. We conducted our experiments on the Breast Cancer Histopathological Database (BreakHis) [14]. It contained 7909 microscopic images of breast tumor tissue, extracted using magnification factors 40X, 100X, 200X and 400X, with approximately 2000 images per magnification factor. Each image had the dimensionality of 700×460 pixels and an associated binary label, indicating whether the sample was benign or malignant. At each magnification factor the data was randomly divided into 5 folds, with approximately 70% of the samples

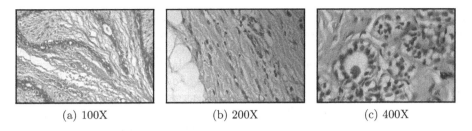

(a) 100X   (b) 200X   (c) 400X

Fig. 1. Sample images from BreakHis dataset at different magnification factors.

reserved for training, and 30% for testing. In our experiments we reused the random partitioning provided by the authors of the BreakHis dataset (Fig. 1).

By default, BreakHis dataset displayed the imbalance of approximately 2.0, with the malignant samples belonging to the majority class. During our experiments we performed undersampling of the data up to the point of achieving the desired imbalance ratio (IR). We considered IRs $\in \{1.0, 2.0, \ldots, 10.0\}$. Importantly, for each IR we used the same total number of samples, that is 676 training and 336 test images. It was the maximum amount of data allowing us to produce every considered IR. We decided to keep the same total number of samples for each IR, as opposed to decreasing the number of samples from the minority class and keeping the size of the majority class constant. It allowed us to avoid the issue of decreasing amount of data, which could be another factor affecting the classification performance.

Classification. For the classification we used the architecture of a convolutional neural network described in [13]. It consisted of 3 convolutional layers with filter size 5×5 and pooling size 3×3. The first layer used 32 channels and max pooling, the second layer used 32 channels and average pooling, and the third layer used 64 channels and average pooling. Afterwards, the network used two fully convolutional layers consisting of 64 and 2 channels, respectively. Each layer except the last used ReLU activation function.

For the training we used stochastic gradient descent with learning rate equal to 0.000001, momentum equal to 0.9, weight decay equal to 0.001 and batch size equal to 1. We used cross entropy as a loss function. Training lasted for 40000 iterations. During the training we augmented the images with a random horizontal flip and a random rotation by a multiple of $90°$.

Prior to feeding the image to the network its size was reduced to 350×230. Additionally, a global per-channel mean was subtracted from every image. The network was supplied with a 64×64 image patches. During training they were selected randomly from the image. During evaluation multiple patches were extracted from the underlying image with a stride of 32, as well as a set of all of their possible augmentations. The individual patch predictions were averaged to obtain the final prediction for the whole image.

Strategies of Dealing with Imbalance. Various approaches to dealing with data imbalance have been proposed in the literature. They can be divided into inbuilt mechanisms, which adjust the behavior of existing classifiers to better accommodate for data imbalance, and resampling strategies, in which either some of the majority samples are omitted (undersampling) or new minority samples are created (oversampling) to achieve a balanced training data distribution. In total, we evaluated 8 different strategies of dealing with data imbalance. Weighted loss (W. Loss), a strategy of assigning a weight associated with misclassification of an object based on its class. Specifically, we used a heuristic described in [3], and assigned the class weight as $w_i = \exp(-r_i)$, with r_i indicating the ratio of class i in the training data. Batch balancing (B. Balance), a strategy of randomly selecting an equal number of minority and majority samples for every batch. The batch size was increased to 2 in case of batch balancing strategy. Random oversampling (ROS), a technique of randomly duplicating some of the minority samples up to the point of achieving class balance. SMOTE [2], an approach in which instead of duplicating existing objects, a synthetic minority observations are produced. In this method new observations are generated by interpolating between original observations. CCR [8], an oversampling strategy that uses smaller local translations instead of interpolating between possibly far-away observations. In addition to oversampling, this method translates the existing majority observations to increase their distance from minority class boundary. RBO [7], another translation-based synthetic oversampling technique, that additionally considers the position of majority objects in process of oversampling. Random undersampling (RUS), a technique of randomly selecting only a subset of majority observations. And the Neighborhood Cleaning Rule (NCL) [10], a guided undersampling strategy, in which neighborhood-based approach is used to guide the process of data cleaning.

Evaluation. Since classification accuracy is not an appropriate metric to assess the classification performance in the imbalanced data setting, throughout the conducted experimental study we use five additional metrics: precision, recall, geometric mean (G-mean), F-measure and AUC. More detailed discussion on the choice of performance metrics can be found in [5] and [6].

2.2 The Impact of Data Imbalance on the Classification Performance

The goal of the first experiment was evaluating to what extent data imbalance affects the classification performance. To this end we undersampled the original BreakHis dataset up to the point of achieving the desired imbalance ratio (IR), at the same time keeping the total number of observations from both classes constant. We considered IR $\in \{1.0, 2.0, \ldots, 10.0\}$. Results of this part of the experimental study, averaged over all folds and magnification factors, were presented in Fig. 2. As can be seen, the accuracy is not an appropriate performance metric in the imbalanced data setting: it increases steadily with IR, despite the accompanying decrease in both precision and recall. On the other hand, all of the remaining measures indicate a significant drop in performance, especially for higher values of IR. For instance, for the balanced distributions we observed

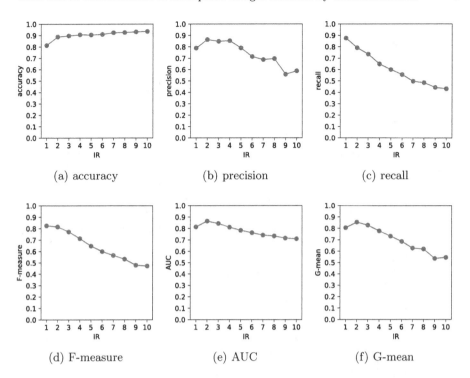

Fig. 2. The impact of data imbalance ratio (IR) on the average values of various performance metrics.

average value of F-measure above 0.8, whereas for the IR $= 10.0$ it drops below 0.5, despite the total number of observations being the same. This indicates that data imbalance has a significant impact on the classifiers behavior and a noticeable decrease in performance can be expected for higher IR. It should be noted that for low values of IR, that is 2 and 3, we actually observed better precision, AUC and G-mean than for the balanced data distribution. This behavior may suggest that depending on our optimization criterion, slight data imbalance can actually be beneficial for the performance of the model. In the case of the histopathological data, especially if the majority class consists of the images of malignant tissue.

2.3 The Evaluation of Strategies of Dealing with Data Imbalance

The goal of the second experiment was comparing various strategies of dealing with data imbalance and assessing which, and under what conditions, lead to the best performance. In this experiment we considered the values of IR $\in \{2.0, 3.0, \ldots, 10.0\}$, and grouped the imbalance into four categories: low (2.0–4.0), medium (5.0–7.0), high (8.0–10.0) and any (2.0–10.0). For each category the results were averaged over the corresponding values of IR. We considered the

Table 1. Average ranks achieved by various techniques of dealing with data imbalance for the specified imbalance ratio (IR). Best performance observed for a given ratio was denoted in bold. The number of times a method achieved statistically significantly better or worse performance than one of the other methods was denoted in subscript with, respectively, a plus or a minus sign.

	IR	Baseline	Inbuilt mechanisms		Oversampling strategies				Undersampling strategies	
			W. Loss	B. Balance	ROS	SMOTE	CCR	RBO	RUS	NCL
Precision	2-4	$\mathbf{1.17}_{+6,-0}$	$2.83_{+4,-0}$	$7.33_{+0,-3}$	$6.42_{+0,-2}$	$4.92_{+0,-1}$	$5.08_{+0,-1}$	$6.42_{+0,-2}$	$7.50_{+0,-3}$	$3.33_{+2,-0}$
	5-7	$\mathbf{2.33}_{+4,-0}$	$4.00_{+0,-0}$	$6.75_{+0,-2}$	$6.83_{+0,-2}$	$4.67_{+0,-0}$	$3.92_{+0,-0}$	$6.50_{+0,-2}$	$7.25_{+0,-2}$	$2.75_{+4,-0}$
	8-10	$\mathbf{3.00}_{+1,-0}$	$3.67_{+1,-0}$	$6.00_{+0,-0}$	$5.58_{+0,-0}$	$5.00_{+0,-0}$	$4.58_{+0,-0}$	$5.83_{+0,-0}$	$7.25_{+0,-2}$	$4.08_{+0,-0}$
	2-10	$\mathbf{2.17}_{+6,-0}$	$3.50_{+4,-0}$	$6.69_{+0,-4}$	$6.28_{+0,-3}$	$4.86_{+1,-1}$	$4.53_{+2,-1}$	$6.25_{+0,-3}$	$7.33_{+0,-5}$	$3.39_{+4,-0}$
Recall	2-4	$8.92_{+0,-6}$	$7.42_{+0,-5}$	$3.83_{+2,-0}$	$3.50_{+2,-0}$	$6.67_{+0,-1}$	$4.00_{+2,-0}$	$3.54_{+2,-0}$	$\mathbf{2.62}_{+3,-0}$	$4.50_{+1,-0}$
	5-7	$8.75_{+0,-5}$	$7.33_{+0,-4}$	$3.54_{+3,-0}$	$2.62_{+3,-0}$	$5.75_{+0,-1}$	$4.38_{+1,-0}$	$\mathbf{2.33}_{+4,-0}$	$3.17_{+3,-0}$	$7.12_{+0,-4}$
	8-10	$8.83_{+0,-5}$	$7.25_{+0,-4}$	$2.88_{+3,-0}$	$3.54_{+3,-0}$	$6.00_{+0,-2}$	$4.83_{+1,-0}$	$2.21_{+4,-0}$	$\mathbf{2.04}_{+4,-0}$	$7.42_{+0,-4}$
	2-10	$8.83_{+0,-7}$	$7.33_{+0,-5}$	$3.42_{+4,-0}$	$3.22_{+4,-0}$	$6.14_{+1,-4}$	$4.40_{+3,-0}$	$2.69_{+4,-0}$	$\mathbf{2.61}_{+4,-0}$	$6.35_{+1,-5}$
F-measure	2-4	$4.25_{+0,-0}$	$3.67_{+0,-0}$	$6.58_{+0,-1}$	$5.50_{+0,-0}$	$5.67_{+0,-0}$	$4.25_{+0,-0}$	$5.33_{+0,-0}$	$7.00_{+0,-1}$	$\mathbf{2.75}_{+2,-0}$
	5-7	$7.17_{+0,-1}$	$6.42_{+0,-0}$	$5.08_{+0,-0}$	$4.25_{+0,-0}$	$4.92_{+0,-0}$	$\mathbf{3.17}_{+1,-0}$	$4.25_{+0,-0}$	$5.08_{+0,-0}$	$4.67_{+0,-0}$
	8-10	$7.33_{+0,-4}$	$5.83_{+0,-0}$	$3.83_{+1,-0}$	$3.67_{+1,-0}$	$5.75_{+0,-0}$	$3.75_{+1,-0}$	$\mathbf{3.42}_{+1,-0}$	$5.08_{+0,-0}$	$6.33_{+0,-0}$
	2-10	$6.25_{+0,-1}$	$5.31_{+0,-0}$	$5.17_{+0,-0}$	$4.47_{+0,-0}$	$5.44_{+0,-0}$	$\mathbf{3.72}_{+1,-0}$	$4.33_{+0,-0}$	$5.72_{+0,-0}$	$4.58_{+0,-0}$
AUC	2-4	$6.50_{+0,-0}$	$4.58_{+0,-0}$	$5.96_{+0,-0}$	$4.58_{+0,-0}$	$5.50_{+0,-0}$	$4.29_{+0,-0}$	$4.67_{+0,-0}$	$5.17_{+0,-0}$	$\mathbf{3.75}_{+0,-0}$
	5-7	$8.75_{+0,-6}$	$7.42_{+0,-4}$	$4.17_{+1,-0}$	$3.17_{+2,-0}$	$5.08_{+1,-0}$	$3.50_{+2,-0}$	$\mathbf{3.12}_{+2,-0}$	$3.33_{+2,-0}$	$6.46_{+0,-0}$
	8-10	$8.58_{+0,-5}$	$7.17_{+0,-4}$	$2.75_{+4,-0}$	$3.42_{+3,-0}$	$6.25_{+0,-3}$	$4.50_{+1,-0}$	$\mathbf{2.33}_{+4,-0}$	$2.67_{+4,-0}$	$7.33_{+0,-4}$
	2-10	$7.94_{+0,-7}$	$6.39_{+0,-5}$	$4.29_{+2,-0}$	$3.72_{+3,-0}$	$5.61_{+1,-1}$	$4.10_{+2,-0}$	$\mathbf{3.38}_{+4,-0}$	$3.72_{+3,-0}$	$5.85_{+1,-3}$
G-mean	2-4	$7.00_{+0,-0}$	$5.42_{+0,-0}$	$5.08_{+0,-0}$	$4.58_{+0,-0}$	$5.92_{+0,-0}$	$4.08_{+0,-0}$	$4.33_{+0,-0}$	$4.67_{+0,-0}$	$\mathbf{3.92}_{+0,-0}$
	5-7	$8.75_{+0,-6}$	$7.58_{+0,-4}$	$4.33_{+1,-0}$	$3.08_{+2,-0}$	$5.33_{+1,-0}$	$3.67_{+2,-0}$	$3.00_{+2,-0}$	$\mathbf{2.92}_{+3,-0}$	$6.33_{+0,-1}$
	8-10	$8.67_{+0,-5}$	$7.33_{+0,-4}$	$2.67_{+4,-0}$	$3.50_{+3,-0}$	$6.25_{+0,-3}$	$4.58_{+1,-0}$	$\mathbf{2.25}_{+4,-0}$	$2.58_{+4,-0}$	$7.17_{+0,-4}$
	2-10	$8.14_{+0,-7}$	$6.78_{+0,-5}$	$4.03_{+2,-0}$	$3.72_{+4,-0}$	$5.83_{+1,-3}$	$4.11_{+2,-0}$	$\mathbf{3.19}_{+4,-0}$	$3.39_{+4,-0}$	$5.81_{+1,-3}$

strategies described in Sect. 2.1, as well as the baseline case, in which no strategy was applied. To assess the statistical significance of the results we performed a Friedman ranking test with a Shaffer post-hoc analysis at the significance level $\alpha = 0.05$. The results were presented in Table 1. As can be seen, there was no single method that achieved best performance on all levels of imbalance and for all of the performance measures. In general, CCR, RBO, RUS and NCL methods achieved the highest rank in at least one of the settings. For low imbalance levels NCL achieved the best performance for all three combined metrics: F-measure, AUC and G-mean. However, in none of the cases did it achieve a statistically significantly better results than the baseline. For higher levels of imbalance RBO achieved the best rank in most cases, with statistically significant differences. While most of the approaches led to an improvement in performance compared to the baseline at least in some settings, two methods, weighted loss and SMOTE, achieved a noticeably worse performance than the other strategies.

2.4   The Value of New Data in the Presence of Data Imbalance

The goal of the third experiment was evaluating to what extent increasing the amount of training data improves the performance for various levels of imbalance. We considered the total number of training observations $\in \{100, 200, \ldots, 600\}$, and IR $\in \{2.0, 4.0, 6.0\}$. In addition to the baseline case, in which no strategy of dealing with imbalance was employed, we used two best-performing resampling techniques: NCL and RBO. The average values of the combined performance measures were presented in Fig. 3. As can be seen, in the baseline case data imbalance decreases the value of new observations. For the case of IR $= 6.0$, even after increasing the number of training samples six times, we did not achieve the same performance as the one observed for IR $= 4.0$, for any of the considered metrics. In other words, even when we used more training data from both minority and majority distributions, due to the inherent data imbalance we achieved a worse performance. To a smaller extent this trend is visible also between IR $= 2.0$ and IR $= 4.0$, especially when F-measure is considered. Using one of the resampling techniques prior to classification partially reduced this trend: in this case, after increasing the number of samples we were able to outperform the case with 100 training samples.

2.5   The Strategy of Balancing Training Distribution During Data Acquisition

In the previous experiments, while adjusting the imbalance ratio we modified both training and test data distributions. However, when dealing with real data we do not have an option of adjusting test distribution. Still, in some cases we can influence the imbalance of training data: for instance, in the case of histopathological images we can have at our disposal a larger quantity of unannotated images, and the main cost is associated with the annotation process. We can, therefore, select the images designed for annotation so that their distribution is balanced. The goal of the final experiment was evaluating whether

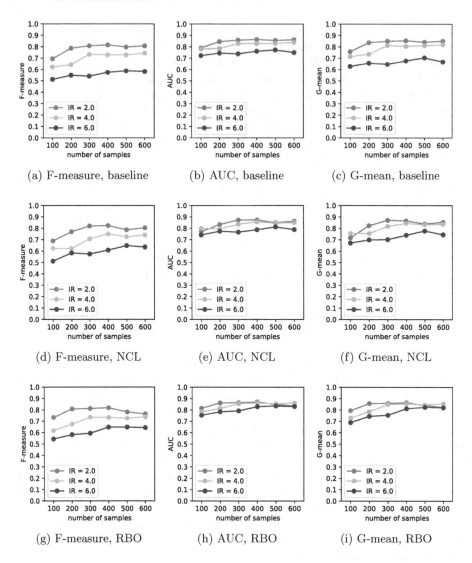

Fig. 3. The impact of the number of training observations on average values of various performance metrics, either on the original data (top row), after undersampling with NCL (middle row) or oversampling with RBO (bottom row).

such data acquisition strategy is beneficial for the classification performance. To this end we evaluated two variants: the baseline case, in which both training and test data distribution were imbalanced with IR $\in \{2.0, 3.0, \ldots, 10.0\}$, and the balanced case, in which only test distribution was imbalanced and training data consisted of an equal number of samples from both classes. We presented the results of this experiment in Fig. 4. For reference, we also included the performance observed on data balanced with NCL and RBO. As can be seen, for

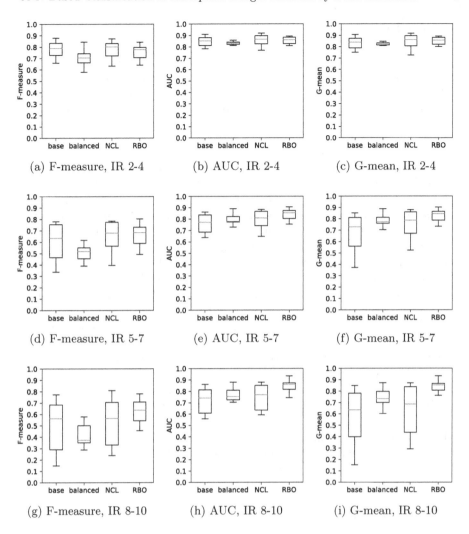

Fig. 4. Average values of various performance metrics. Baseline case, in which both training and test data was imbalanced, was compared with the case in which only test data was imbalanced. Performance for NCL and RBO was also included for reference.

low values of IR we actually observed a worse performance after balancing the training data according to all of the combined performance metrics. This trend was most noticeable for F-measure. Furthermore, the observed F-measure was also higher in the baseline case for higher IR. On the other hand, balancing training data improved the AUC and G-mean for medium and high levels of imbalance. In all of the cases, using the original, imbalanced training data distribution and balancing it with one of the considered resampling strategies led to an improvement in performance.

3 Conclusions

In this paper we experimentally evaluated the impact of data imbalance on the classification performance of convolutional neural network in breast cancer histopathological image recognition task. We conducted our analysis on the Breast Cancer Histopathological Database (BreakHis) [14]. The main findings of our experiments are the following:

- Medium and high data imbalance levels have a significant negative impact on the classification performance, irregardless of the chosen performance measure. However, for some of the considered measures, at low level of imbalance we observed an improved performance, which may suggest that small data imbalance can actually be beneficial in a specific settings. Especially the latter finding should be further confirmed on additional benchmark datasets.
- Some of the popular strategies of dealing with data imbalance, namely using weighted loss and oversampling data with SMOTE, significantly underperformed in the conducted experiments. Techniques that achieved the best results were NCL and RBO resampling algorithms. This leads us to a conclusion that developing a novel strategies of handling data imbalance, designed specifically for dealing with images, might be necessary to achieve a satisfactory performance in the histopathological image recognition task.
- Data imbalance negatively impacts the value of additional training data. Even when more data from both minority and majority class was used, due to data imbalance we were unable to achieve a performance observed for lower imbalance ratios. This can be partially mitigated by using an appropriate strategy of handling data imbalance.
- Depending on data imbalance ratio and the metric used to measure classification performance, balancing training data during acquisition can have a negative impact on the performance when compared to sampling training data with the same imbalance ratio as test data. In all of the considered cases, applying resampling on imbalanced data was preferable approach to balancing data during acquisition.

Since the conducted analysis based on a single benchmark dataset, further research should be focused on extending it to additional databases. Furthermore, a limited number of already proposed strategies dedicated to dealing with image imbalance should be included in the method comparison. Design of a novel methods is also likely necessary to be able to achieve a satisfactory performance.

Acknowledgment. This research was supported by the National Science Centre, Poland, under the grant no. 2017/27/N/ST6/01705 and the PLGrid infrastructure.

References

1. Buda, M., Maki, A., Mazurowski, M.A.: A systematic study of the class imbalance problem in convolutional neural networks. arXiv preprint arXiv:1710.05381 (2017)
2. Chawla, N.V., Bowyer, K.W., Hall, L.O., Kegelmeyer, W.P.: SMOTE: synthetic minority over-sampling technique. J. Artif. Intell. Res. **16**, 321–357 (2002)
3. Dong, Q., Gong, S., Zhu, X.: Imbalanced deep learning by minority class incremental rectification. arXiv preprint arXiv:1804.10851 (2018)
4. Hamidinekoo, A., Denton, E., Rampun, A., Honnor, K., Zwiggelaar, R.: Deep learning in mammography and breast histology, an overview and future trends. Med. Image Anal. **47**, 45–67 (2018)
5. He, H., Garcia, E.A.: Learning from imbalanced data. IEEE Trans. Knowl. Data Eng. **21**(9), 1263–1284 (2009)
6. Japkowicz, N., Shah, M.: Evaluating Learning Algorithms: A Classification Perspective. Cambridge University Press, Cambridge (2011)
7. Koziarski, M., Krawczyk, B., Woźniak, M.: Radial-based approach to imbalanced data oversampling. In: Martínez de Pisón, F.J., Urraca, R., Quintián, H., Corchado, E. (eds.) HAIS 2017. LNCS (LNAI), vol. 10334, pp. 318–327. Springer, Cham (2017). https://doi.org/10.1007/978-3-319-59650-1_27
8. Koziarski, M., Woźniak, M.: CCR: a combined cleaning and resampling algorithm for imbalanced data classification. Int. J. Appl. Math. Comput. Sci. **27**(4), 727–736 (2017)
9. Krawczyk, B.: Learning from imbalanced data: open challenges and future directions. Prog. Artif. Intell. **5**(4), 221–232 (2016)
10. Laurikkala, J.: Improving identification of difficult small classes by balancing class distribution. In: Quaglini, S., Barahona, P., Andreassen, S. (eds.) AIME 2001. LNCS (LNAI), vol. 2101, pp. 63–66. Springer, Heidelberg (2001). https://doi.org/10.1007/3-540-48229-6_9
11. Lusa, L., et al.: SMOTE for high-dimensional class-imbalanced data. BMC Bioinform. **14**(1), 106 (2013)
12. Pulgar, F.J., Rivera, A.J., Charte, F., del Jesus, M.J.: On the impact of imbalanced data in convolutional neural networks performance. In: Martínez de Pisón, F.J., Urraca, R., Quintián, H., Corchado, E. (eds.) HAIS 2017. LNCS (LNAI), vol. 10334, pp. 220–232. Springer, Cham (2017). https://doi.org/10.1007/978-3-319-59650-1_19
13. Spanhol, F.A., Oliveira, L.S., Petitjean, C., Heutte, L.: Breast cancer histopathological image classification using convolutional neural networks. In: 2016 International Joint Conference on Neural Networks (IJCNN), pp. 2560–2567. IEEE (2016)
14. Spanhol, F.A., Oliveira, L.S., Petitjean, C., Heutte, L.: A dataset for breast cancer histopathological image classification. IEEE Trans. Biomed. Eng. **63**(7), 1455–1462 (2016)

Three-Stream Convolution Networks
After Background Subtraction
for Action Recognition

Chao Li[✉][iD] and Yue Ming

Beijing University of Posts and Telecommunications, Beijing, China
{lichaovortex,yming}@bupt.edu.cn

Abstract. Action recognition has vital significance for computer vision. Recently, deep learning has made breakthrough progress in action recognition. However, as two important branches of deep learning, Two-Stream relies on optical flow with complex computation and 3D convolution network is difficult for training. In this paper, we propose a novel Three-Stream Convolution networks after feature extraction for action recognition. For feature, we introduce three input features: RGB images, background subtraction feature with low complexity and historical contour feature. In order to optimize the discriminability of long-term actions, the historical contour feature is superimposed by background subtraction feature. For network structure, we present a convolution network stream for each feature input: RGB net, background subtraction sequence net and historical contour net. Finally, we merge three streams into one network with automatic network learning mechanism for action recognition to obtain a better recognition performance. We conduct experiments on two large main action recognition datasets UCF-101 and HMDB-51. Comparing the mainstream methods, the results verify the accuracy and high efficiency of our framework.

Keywords: Three-Stream · Background subtraction · Action recognition · Fusion network · Convolution

1 Introduction

Action recognition, is a crucial and challenging task in the field of video analysis which has significant timing correlation. However, the performance will drop significantly under background noise. Therefore, how to focus on the action itself and extract effective timing features become the key to the research of action recognition. Recently, CNN has achieved excellent performance on many applications in computer vision, including action recognition. Currently, mainstream deep CNN for action recognition is based on the two frameworks: Two Stream framework [1] and 3D convolution network [2] framework. Two Stream framework fuses original RGB images and dense optical flow sequence images with two networks, while 3D convolution network framework expands the dimensions of original convolution network so that it can capture the timing related feature. However, the extraction of dense optical flow need complex computation. In

X. Bai et al. (Eds.): FFER 2018/DLPR 2018, LNCS 11264, pp. 12–24, 2019.
https://doi.org/10.1007/978-3-030-12177-8_2

addition, 3D convolution network is difficult to train owing to its large amount of parameters and cannot capture the discriminability of long-term sequence (Fig. 1).

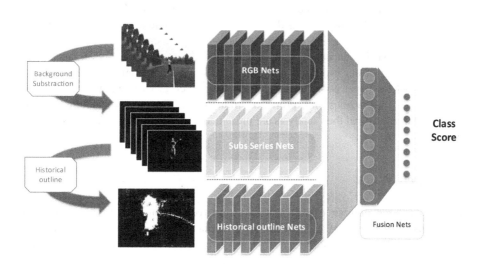

Fig. 1. Three-Stream convolution networks after background subtraction includes three streams: RGB net (with original RGB images), background subtraction sequence net (with background subtraction feature sequence) and historical contour net (with historical contour feature images). Fusion net fuses 3 streams' information in the end to obtain a better performance. (Color figure online)

In this paper, we propose Three-Stream Convolution networks after background subtraction for action recognition. At present, optical flow is the main description method of motion feature and the apparent invariance of the action target. However, it is limited by its slow speed of extraction. In order to extract better action discriminant feature, we introduce the background subtraction feature, which is the binarization feature obtained from original images and has the fast extraction speed and motion description. In addition, the background subtraction feature introduces the attention mechanism to focus more on the action itself without the background interference. For some long-term action, short time feature is difficult to describe. We set different sampling time intervals for whole image sequence and superimpose long-term background subtraction feature into historical contour image which can capture the long-term action. Then, we take the original RGB image, the image sequence after the background subtraction and the historical contour image as input, and train three streams to learn three different features. Finally, we merge the three streams into one fusion network with automatic network learning mechanism for action recognition, which is an end-to-end network. Our entire framework significantly improves the speed of feature extraction.

The main contribution of our proposed framework is that we have explored the feature description for action. We introduce background subtraction feature as input to the CNN which it significantly improves the feature extraction speed of the framework.

Meanwhile, we utilize the time interval sampling method to superimpose the background subtraction feature into a historical contour image, optimizing the discriminate action. In addition, we merge three streams into one fusion end-to-end framework for action recognition. We conducted extensive experiments on HMDB-51 dataset [3] and UCF-101 dataset [4], and the results show the effectiveness of our Three-Stream convolution networks in action recognition. Comparing the current main methods, our proposed framework balances the computation and the recognition performance. The feature extraction of our proposed framework has lower computational complexity.

The rest of the paper is organized as follows. In Sect. 2, we summarize the related work. Section 3 describes our proposed framework. The implementation details, experimental results and their analysis are presented in Sect. 4. Finally, conclusions are drawn in Sect. 5.

2   Related Work

There are a large number of research in action recognition with deep convolution network recently. Current works of deep learning mainly consist of two aspects: feature extraction and network model.

2.1   Feature Extraction

In action recognition, the works on the input mainly includes RGB images inputs and video sequence. There are a large amount of works focusing on hand-engineered feature, which can capture the appearance and motion information from frames in videos, such as HOG3D [5], SIFT3D [6], HOF [7], ESURF [8], MBH [9], IDTs [10], and so on. The input format of the spatial stream is usually a single RGB image or a multi-frame RGB sequence. However, the multi-frame RGB sequence contains a large number of redundant frames. In order to reduce the number of spatial input channels, a large number of works focus on the method of selecting images before input, such as Key Volume Mining Deep Framework [11]. In addition, the adascan framework [12] raises the accuracy of classification by extracting key frames in the video and it selects key frames automatically during convolution layers or pooling layers in the convolution network. For the temporal inputs, the main works focus on the improvement of the optical flow feature. Flownet [13] and Hidden Two-Stream [14] both learn the optical flow feature with the network, which is designed to improve the quality of the optical flow and reduce the extraction time of the optical flow. However, whether the optical flow feature is the optimal motion auxiliary feature is uncertain and it needs complex computation. How to train the better motion feature instead of the optical flow feature is one of the next trends, which is exactly what our work explored.

2.2   Network Model

In deep learning, the convolution network is introduced into the action to extract features. It is mainly divided into two main network frameworks: Two-Stream CNN network [1] and 3D convolution network [2]. The Two-Stream CNN network is designed as two parts. One part deals with RGB images and the other deals with optical flow feature. Then, two streams obtain joint training and classification. The improved work based on Two-Stream network mainly focuses on the selection of key frames [11, 15] and the deeper convolution network [16]. In addition, some work [17] focus on the study of different fusion between networks in two stream to obtain the better fusion result. 3D convolution network is another major mainstream method in deep learning. Although the current 3D convolution network's accuracy does not exceed Two-Stream framework, it is much faster and it is an end to end training framework. 3D convolution is based on two dimensional convolution network and introduces description of timing variability. The work of 3D convolution mainly focuses on the improvement of network structure. I3D [18] from DeepID introduces the 3D convolution network that is based on Inception-V1 [19]. T3D [20] proposes 3D dense net and TTL layer which uses different scales of convolution to capture the feature. P3D [21] improves the 3D Resnet to obtain an extreme deep network, which improved the discriminability of action. These work is all based on large datasets, which need a large number of computing and storage resource of computer. By contrast, our proposed framework is easier for training.

3   Our Method

In this Section, we will introduce the details of our proposed Three-Stream convolution network, which mainly includes the feature extraction and Three-Stream network model.

3.1   Feature Extraction

Our feature extraction method is based on background subtraction. First, we convert the original video into an RGB image sequence. Secondly, we utilize background subtraction of the RGB sequence to obtain the background subtraction feature sequence, as shown in Fig. 2. Thirdly, a historical contour image is obtained by sampling and superimposing the background subtraction feature sequence.

We use the background modeling method based on mixed Gaussian model [22] to complete background subtraction. There is still a certain degree of noise in the processed image obtained by background subtraction. In order to remove the influence of noise, we expand the denoising process to the image after background subtraction.

In action recognition, multi-frame RGB images are taken as input to push the network learn inter-frame changes through the information in different times. The convolution network has excellent feature extraction capability for the spatial texture features of the still image, but it is difficult to directly extract the feature of the combination of time series and space from multi frame images. The background subtraction feature removes effectively background interference and unrelated texture features which can effectively learn inter frame changing information and it preserves the motion information and contour information of the action target (as shown in Fig. 3). Background subtraction will reduce the difficulty of learning the network timing feature. The background extraction feature is fast and does not consume much time in our whole framework.

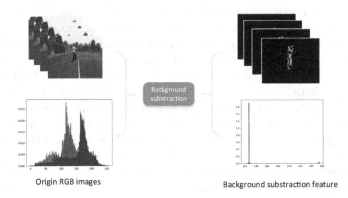

Origin RGB images   Background substraction feature

Fig. 2. Background subtraction. The images processed with background subtraction only keep the information related to the action target. The right column shows changes in histogram.

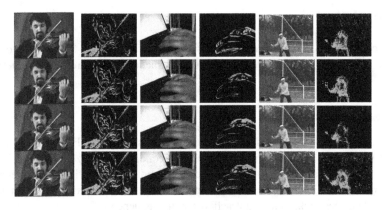

Fig. 3. Examples of UCF-101 dataset with background subtraction. (playing violin, typing and tenis swing).

Since the input to the convolutional network is fixed, continuous short-time frames inputs are difficult to describe the discrimination of long-term actions. It is difficult to obtain significant recognition results simply by increasing the number of input frames. Therefore, in order to better describe the inter-class relationships of long-term actions, we sampled the original background subtraction sequence according to the time interval. Then we calculate the maximum value of the pixel at each position for each frame of image pixels to obtain the historical contour image feature. Finally, we binarized the historical contour image to obtain a more concise description.

We superimpose background subtraction features into historical contour feature which assists in adding long-term actions discriminability. Meanwhile, since the historical contour image can be superimposed by any number of frames, the convolution network can learn any long-scale information so that the performance of long-term scale action recognition can be further optimized. The specific framework of super-imposing is shown in Fig. 4.

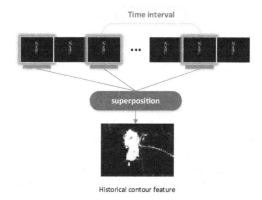

Fig. 4. Historical contour image sampling framework. Background subtraction features are superimposed into historical contour image.

Based on the analysis and processing mentioned above, we propose three kinds of feature to learn, namely: original RGB images, background subtraction feature and historical contour image. Therefore, our framework covers the original RGB information, action motion information and long-term scale contour information.

3.2 Three-Sream Convolution

Our proposed Three-Stream convolution network improves the structure of Two-Stream convolutional network [1]. Our network structure is divided into four parts: RGB net, background subtraction sequence net, historical contour net and Fusion net, as shown in Fig. 5.

The input of RGB net is randomly selected from the image sequence. The design of network is based on the residual structure [23]. The first two layers are convolution of kernel 3 * 3, and the rest part is composed of res-block. RGB net mainly extracts the texture and appearance feature from the RGB image. The input of the background subtraction net is background subtraction feature according to the time order. The main structure of the network is the same as RGB net. The background subtraction sequence net mainly learns the motion feature of action and contour feature of the action target. The historical contour net's input is the historical contour image. Due to the small number of historical contour images, the recognition network is smaller than other streams. The historical contour net mainly learns the contour feature of long-term scale action for improving the performance. Fusion net merge three streams into one network to obtain the classification scores.

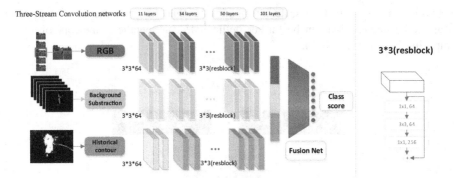

Fig. 5. Three-Stream convolution networks includes three streams: RGB net (with original RGB images), background subtraction sequence net (with background subtraction feature sequence) and historical contour net (with historical contour image). Fusion nets fuses 3 streams' information in the end to extract the discrimination more effectively. We test four scales deep networks, which are 11, 34, 50, 101. The right is the bottleneck structure [23].

There are two methods for fusion: average fusion and network fusion. We define the feature map from streams as $I_S(w, h, c)$. Here w and h is the width and height of the feature map, and c is the channels of the feature map. The s is one stream of the three streams. We use fully connected layer to obtain the classification scores. We learn the mapping from the feature extracted by stream to classification scores f, and classification scores can be described as:

$$cl_s = f[I_S(w, h, c)] \qquad (1)$$

For average fusion, each stream has the same weight, so the fusion can be described as:

$$Cl_{ave} = \sum_{s=1}^{3} \sum_{i=1}^{n} cl_s(i) \qquad (2)$$

where n denotes the classes of recognition. Setting value manually cannot obtain the best performance, so we utilize the automatic network learning mechanism. Therefore, we concatenate the feature extracted from the three streams and input into the fully connected network, which can be described as:

$$Cl_f(N) = f[I_1(w, h, c), I_2(w, h, c), I_3(w, h, c)] \qquad (3)$$

Therefore, we merge three streams into one fusion network and it completes the end-to-end action recognition framework. We conducted extensive experiments to test the effectiveness of our network in action recognition.

4   Experiments

In this section, we first describe the evaluation data set and implementation details of our framework. Then we compare the performance with the current state-of-the-art methods.

4.1   Datasets and Implementation Details

We conduct experiments and methods evaluation on two large action recognition datasets UCF-101 [4] and HMDB-51 [3], which are the mainstream datasets in the field of video action recognition. With 13320 videos from 101 action categories, UCF101 gives the largest diversity in terms of actions and with the presence of large variations in camera motion, object appearance and pose, object scale, viewpoint, cluttered background, illumination conditions, etc., it is the most challenging data set to date. HMDB-51 is collected from various sources, mostly from movies, and a small proportion from public databases such as the Prelinger archive, YouTube and Google videos. The dataset contains 6849 clips divided into 51 action categories, each containing a minimum of 101 clips. First, we convert the original video set into images sequence. Then, we further transform images into a background subtraction feature images and historical contour image. The evaluation protocol [3] is the same for both datasets: the organizers provide three splits into training and test data, and the performance is measured by the mean classification accuracy across the splits. In addition, the server we used for the experiment is equipped with two Titan X GPUs and a E5-2620 CPU.

4.2   Experiments of Feature Extraction

We test the performance of proposed extracted feature inputted to the convolution network in different layers, as shown in Table 1. In experiments, we select a random RGB image for each video and related background subtraction feature images as inputs for our proposed framework.

Table 1. Evaluation results of RGB and RGB with background subtraction feature (B. Subtraction+RGB). Trained and tested on UCF-101. All models are trained from scratch.

Method	Network	Top1	Top5
RGB	Resnet18	70.71%	91.41%
RGB	Resnet34	74.94%	91.67%
RGB	Resnet50	76.13%	93.81%
RGB	Resnet101	78.48%	94.50%
B.Substraction+RGB	Resnet18	79.65%	94.45%
B.Substraction+RGB	Resnet34	81.39%	95.29%
B.Substraction+RGB	Resnet50	82.24%	95.98%
B.Substraction+RGB	Resnet101	84.56%	96.83%

As the number of layer increases, the recognition performance significantly improves. The results indicate that the performance of the RGB and background subtraction feature in action recognition is significantly improved comparing with the original RGB, which verifies effectiveness of the background subtraction feature in our framework.

We further compare the extraction speed of the background subtraction feature and the optical flow feature. We use Mog2 [22] background subtraction algorithm and compare the speed with Flownet [13] and other methods of optical flow, as shown in Table 2. For matrix computation, the computing speed of GPU is much faster than CPU. Table 2 shows that the extraction speed of the optical flow in GPU is much lower than that of the background subtraction algorithm in CPU, which verifies the advantages of our proposed framework in the input feature extraction speed.

Table 2. The comparison of the extraction speed (Background subtraction and optical flow methods)

Method	CPU (fps)	GPU (fps)
B.Substraction	167	–
Flownet [13]	–	1.12
Epicflow [24]	0.063	–
Deepflow [25]	0.058	–
EPPM [26]	–	5
LDOF [27]	0.015	0.4

There are a large number of redundant frames in the action video list which does not benefit the results and increase the burden of operation. Therefore, when superimposing the background subtraction feature into historical contour image, we sample the background subtraction feature sequence according to the time. And we set different time interval for optimal sampling strategy when generating the historical contour image, as shown in Fig. 6. We evaluate four time intervals of 5, 10, 15, and 20.

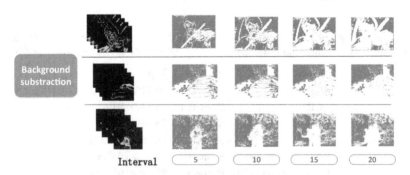

Fig. 6. Different time intervals of 5, 10, 15, and 20. Examples of UCF-101 dataset with historical contour feature. (playing violin, typing and tennis swing)

Different time intervals determine the sparseness of the generated historical contour image which intuitively indicates the continuity of the description by increasing time interval gradually. Too large time intervals will lose the key information of the action, while too small time intervals cannot improve the performance, as shown in Table 3. For action recognition, selecting the appropriate time interval can maximize the recognition performance.

Table 3. Evaluation results of our Three-Stream framework. Trained and tested on ucf-101 split 1. All models are trained from scratch.

Method	Network	Interval	UCF-101
Three Stream	Resnet101	5	84.46%
Three Stream	Resnet101	10	84.58%
Three Stream	*Resnet101*	*15*	*84.92%*
Three Stream	Resnet101	20	84.74%
Three Stream	Resnet18	15	80.01%
Three Stream	Resnet34	15	81.99%
Three Stream	Resnet50	15	82.80%

In experiments, different time intervals mean that the corresponding frames are skipped during the superposition. The result of experiment shows that when time interval is 15, the performance of our proposed framework is the more effective. Therefore, we set time interval to 15 in next experiments for better recognition performance. It can be seen from Table 3 there is a small improvement in performance. We believe that there should be more improvement if the dataset contains more long-term data.

4.3   Evaluation of Three-Stream

We train RGB net, background subtraction sequence net and historical contour net as three streams, then merge three streams into one network. The results of our comparison with state-of-the-art methods are shown in Table 4.

Table 4. Evaluation results of our proposed framework on UCF-101 and HMDB. All models are trained from scratch.

Method	UCF-101	HMDB
C3D [2]	82.30%	–
Conv Fusion [28]	82.60%	56.80%
DT+MVSV [29]	83.5	55.90%
Idt+FV [10]	85.90%	57.20%
Conv Pooling [30]	82.60%	47.10%
Spatial Stream-Resnet [31]	82.30%	43.40%
Two-Stream CNN (101)	87.76%	58.00%
Hidden Two-Stream [14]	88.70%	58.90%
3D-ResNet [16]	84.21%	57.33%
(Ours)Three-Stream-18	80.01%	52.57%
(Ours)Three-Stream-34	81.99%	53.36%
(Ours)Three-Stream-50	82.80%	55.58%
(Ours)Three-Stream-101	84.92%	56.51%

Here we can see from Table 4 that we obtain the performance similar to Two-Stream (RGB+Optical Flow) with different layers of the network. Based on these results, our proposed framework balances the computation and the recognition performance. The feature extraction of our framework has lower computational complexity with the close the recognition performance.

5 Conclusion

In this paper, we propose Three-Stream Convolution networks after background subtraction for action recognition. Three kinds of extracted features are inputted in our framework: original RGB images, background subtraction feature and historical contour image. Then we merge RGB net, background subtraction sequence net and historical contour net into one network automatically learning the fusion feature to obtain a better recognition performance. Therefore, our framework covers the original RGB information, action motion information and long-term scale contour information. The feature extraction of our proposed framework has lower computational complexity comparing with the current methods. We conduct experiments on two large main action recognition datasets UCF-101 and HMDB-51 and the results verify the accuracy and high efficiency of our framework. We will explore more effective framework in action recognition in the future.

Acknowledgment. This work was supported by the National Natural Science Foundation of China (Grants No. 6140204), Beijing Natural Science Foundation (Grants No. 4172024).

References

1. Simonyan, K., Zisserman, A.: Two-stream convolutional networks for action recognition in videos. In: Advances in Neural Information Processing Systems, pp. 568–576 (2014)
2. Ji, S., Xu, W., Yang, M., Yu, K.: 3D convolutional neural networks for human action recognition. IEEE Trans. Pattern Anal. Mach. Intell. **35**(1), 221–231 (2013)
3. Jhuang, H., Garrote, H., Poggio, E., Serre, T., Hmdb, T.: A large video database for human motion recognition. In: Proceedings of IEEE International Conference on Computer Vision, vol. 4, p. 6 (2011)
4. Soomro, K., Zamir, A.R., Shah, M.: UCF101: a dataset of 101 human actions classes from videos in the wild. arXiv preprint arXiv:1212.0402 (2012)
5. Klaser, A., Marszałek, M., Schmid, C.: A spatio-temporal descriptor based on 3D-gradients. In: BMVC 2008-19th British Machine Vision Conference, p. 275-1. British Machine Vision Association (2008)
6. Scovanner, P., Ali, S., Shah, M.: A 3-dimensional sift descriptor and its application to action recognition. In: Proceedings of the 15th ACM International Conference on Multimedia, pp. 357–360. ACM (2007)
7. Laptev, I., Marszałek, M., Schmid, C., Rozenfeld, B.: Learning realistic human actions from movies. In: IEEE Conference on Computer Vision and Pattern Recognition, CVPR 2008, pp. 1–8. IEEE (2008)

8. Willems, G., Tuytelaars, T., Van Gool, L.: An efficient dense and scale-invariant spatio-temporal interest point detector. In: Forsyth, D., Torr, P., Zisserman, A. (eds.) ECCV 2008. LNCS, vol. 5303, pp. 650–663. Springer, Heidelberg (2008). https://doi.org/10.1007/978-3-540-88688-4_48

9. Dalal, N., Triggs, B., Schmid, C.: Human detection using oriented histograms of flow and appearance. In: Leonardis, A., Bischof, H., Pinz, A. (eds.) ECCV 2006. LNCS, vol. 3952, pp. 428–441. Springer, Heidelberg (2006). https://doi.org/10.1007/11744047_33

10. Wang, H., Schmid, C.: Action recognition with improved trajectories. In: Proceedings of the IEEE International Conference on Computer Vision, pp. 3551–3558 (2013)

11. Zhu, W., Hu, J., Sun, G., Cao, X., Qiao, Y.: A key volume mining deep framework for action recognition. In: Proceedings of the IEEE Conference on Computer Vision and Pattern Recognition, pp. 1991–1999 (2016)

12. Kar, A., Rai, N., Sikka, K., Sharma, G.: AdaScan: adaptive scan pooling in deep convolutional neural networks for human action recognition in videos. In: The IEEE Conference on Computer Vision and Pattern Recognition (CVPR), vol. 2 (2017)

13. Dosovitskiy, A., et al.: FlowNet: learning optical flow with convolutional networks. In: Proceedings of the IEEE International Conference on Computer Vision, pp. 2758–2766 (2015)

14. Zhu, Y., Lan, Z., Newsam, S., Hauptmann, A.G.: Hidden two-stream convolutional networks for action recognition. arXiv preprint arXiv:1704.00389 (2017)

15. Wang, L., et al.: Temporal segment networks: towards good practices for deep action recognition. In: Leibe, B., Matas, J., Sebe, N., Welling, M. (eds.) ECCV 2016. LNCS, vol. 9912, pp. 20–36. Springer, Cham (2016). https://doi.org/10.1007/978-3-319-46484-8_2

16. Hara, K., Kataoka, H., Satoh, Y.: Can spatiotemporal 3D CNNs retrace the history of 2D CNNs and ImageNet. In: Proceedings of the IEEE Conference on Computer Vision and Pattern Recognition, Salt Lake City, UT, USA, pp. 18–22 (2018)

17. Feichtenhofer, C., Pinz, A., Wildes, R.P.: Spatiotemporal multiplier networks for video action recognition. In: 2017 IEEE Conference on Computer Vision and Pattern Recognition (CVPR), pp. 7445–7454. IEEE (2017)

18. Carreira, J., Zisserman, A.: Quo Vadis, action recognition? A new model and the kinetics dataset. In: 2017 IEEE Conference on Computer Vision and Pattern Recognition (CVPR), pp. 4724–4733. IEEE (2017)

19. Szegedy, C., et al.: Going deeper with convolutions. In: Proceedings of the IEEE Conference on Computer Vision and Pattern Recognition, pp. 1–9 (2015)

20. Diba, A., et al.: Temporal 3D convnets: new architecture and transfer learning for video classification. arXiv preprint arXiv:1711.08200 (2017)

21. Li, Q., Qiu, Z., Yao, T., Mei, T., Rui, Y., Luo, J.: Action recognition by learning deep multi-granular spatio-temporal video representation. In: Proceedings of the 2016 ACM on International Conference on Multimedia Retrieval, pp. 159–166. ACM (2016)

22. Zivkovic, Z.: Improved adaptive gaussian mixture model for background subtraction. In: Proceedings of the 17th International Conference on Pattern Recognition, ICPR 2004, vol. 2, pp. 28–31. IEEE (2004)

23. He, K., Zhang, X., Ren, S., Sun, J.: Deep residual learning for image recognition. In: Proceedings of the IEEE Conference on Computer Vision and Pattern Recognition, pp. 770–778 (2016)

24. Revaud, J., Weinzaepfel, P., Harchaoui, Z., Schmid, C.: EpicFlow: edge-preserving interpolation of correspondences for optical flow. In: Proceedings of the IEEE Conference on Computer Vision and Pattern Recognition, pp. 1164–1172 (2015)

25. Weinzaepfel, P., Revaud, J., Harchaoui, Z., Schmid, C.: DeepFlow: large displacement optical flow with deep matching. In: Proceedings of the IEEE International Conference on Computer Vision, pp. 1385–1392 (2013)
26. Bao, L., Yang, Q., Jin, H.: Fast edge-preserving patchmatch for large displacement optical flow. In: Proceedings of the IEEE Conference on Computer Vision and Pattern Recognition, pp. 3534–3541 (2014)
27. Brox, T., Malik, J.: Large displacement optical flow: descriptor matching in variational motion estimation. IEEE Trans. Pattern Anal. Mach. Intell. **33**(3), 500–513 (2011)
28. Feichtenhofer, C., Pinz, A., Zisserman, A.: Convolutional two-stream network fusion for video action recognition. In: Proceedings of the IEEE Conference on Computer Vision and Pattern Recognition, pp. 1933–1941 (2016)
29. Cai, Z., Wang, L., Peng, X., Qiao, Y.: Multi-view super vector for action recognition. In: Proceedings of the IEEE Conference on Computer Vision and Pattern Recognition, pp. 596–603 (2014)
30. Yue-Hei Ng, J., Hausknecht, M., Vijayanarasimhan, S., Vinyals, O., Monga, R., Toderici, G.: Beyond short snippets: deep networks for video classification. In: Proceedings of the IEEE Conference on Computer Vision and Pattern Recognition, pp. 4694–4702 (2015)
31. Feichtenhofer, C., Pinz, A., Wildes, R.: Spatiotemporal residual networks for video action recognition. In: Advances in Neural Information Processing Systems, pp. 3468–3476 (2016)

Scene Text Detection with a SSD and Encoder-Decoder Network Based Method

Cong Luo[1] and Xue Gao[1,2(✉)]

[1] School of Electronic and Information Engineering,
South China University of Technology, Guangzhou, China
xuegao@scut.edu.cn
[2] SCUT-Zhuhai Institute of Modern Industrial Innovation, Zhuhai, China

Abstract. In this work, we propose a simple yet powerful method that yields effective text detection in natural scenes. We present a Text Localization Neural Network, which detects text in scene images with one forward propagation and a standard non-maximum suppression subsequently. In order to eliminate few scene background mistaken by Text Localization Neural Network, we propose a Text Verification Model based on the encoder-decoder network. Thus, precision of text detection can be further improved by recognizing text in our candidate text regions. We have evaluated the proposed method for text detection on our own constructed horizontal text detection dataset. Compared with previous approaches, our method achieves a highest recall rate of 0.784 and competitive precision rate in text detection.

Keywords: Text detection · SSD · Encoder-decoder network

1 Introduction

Text detection, usually as a first step in text reading systems, which aims at localize text regions with bounding boxes of words, play a critical role in the whole procedure of text information extraction and understanding. Although there are some OCR systems for documental texts, detecting text in natural scenes is still a challenge due to complex background, various font sizes and colors, etc.

While text in natural scenes can be regarded as a kind of specific target, we propose in this work a novel method for natural scene text detection. Our method is based on Single Shot MultiBox Detector (SSD) [1] and encoder-decoder network, the whole procedure of our text detection method is illustrated in Fig. 1.

We present Text Localization Neural Network based on SSD, which is designed for initial text candidates localization with single forward pass as well as a standard Non-Maximum Suppression. We also propose a Text Verification Model based on encoder-decoder network, which further improve the precision of text detection by eliminating background of initial detection results.

© Springer Nature Switzerland AG 2019
X. Bai et al. (Eds.): FFER 2018/DLPR 2018, LNCS 11264, pp. 25–34, 2019.
https://doi.org/10.1007/978-3-030-12177-8_3

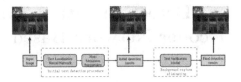

Fig. 1. Overview for our text detection procedure. Whole procedure mainly takes two steps: 1. Initial text detection with Text Localization Neural Network. 2. Eliminating background regions with Text Verification Model.

Specifically, we construct a text detection dataset taken by camera in natural scenes and from RCTW [2] dataset. Experiments show the proposed method achieves a highest recall rate of 0.784 and competitive precision rate compared with other approaches.

In summary, the contributions of this paper are three-folds: (1) We propose a Text Localization Neural Network based on SSD, which may better suit the problem of scene text detection. (2) We design a Text Verification Model based on encoder-decoder network, precision improvement can be made by making use of text recognition results to eliminate background regions. (3) We test the effectiveness of our method by conducting experiments on our scene text detection dataset.

2   Related Work

Detecting text in natural scenes has been a hot research topic in the field of computer vision, and plenty of excellent works and effective strategies has been proposed. Previous works on text detection mainly seek text instances with sliding-window [3–5] or connected component extraction [6–9] techniques. Sliding-window based methods detect text by looking over all possible regions of text, which may achieve considerable recall rate at the cost of heavy computations. Connected component extraction based methods may extract candidate text with much lower computation cost firstly, post-processing steps of candidates filtering are unavoidable. Stroke Width Transform (SWT) [6] and Maximally Stable Extremal Regions (MSER) [9] are two representable algorithms with leading performance in ICDAR 2011 [10] and ICDAR 2013 [11]. Yao et al. [8] seek candidate text with the help of SWT, and design a multi-oriented text detection algorithm combined with region color and shape features. Sun et al. [12] proposed color enhancement extremal regions based on MSER for candidate text generation.

Deep learning technologies have advanced performance of text detection in the past years. A technique similar to text detection is general object detection. Owing to rapid development of deep object detection networks, horizontal scene text detection can be realized based on those networks. Huang et al. [13] firstly seek candidate text via MSER, CNN is then used to classify text/non-text regions. Based on Faster R-CNN [14], DeepText [15] proposed Inception-RPN

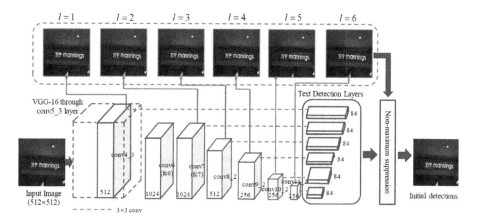

Fig. 2. Structure of Text Localization Neural Network. The network is a 28-layer fully convolutional network, one part is a 13-layer base network inherited from VGG-16, another part is composed of 15 extra convolution layers. Six extra Text Detection Layers are responsible for prediction of scene text. Green rectangular boxes are examples of size increasing default text bounding boxes among different feature layers. (Color figure online)

and made further optimization to adapt text detection. Tian et al. [16] designed a network called Connectionist Text Proposal Network (CTPN), which combined CNN and LSTM to detect text line by predicting a sequence of fine-scale text components. Inspired by YOLO [17], Gupta et al. [18] proposed a fully convolutional regression network, which made predictions through a single forward pass. On the other hand, text detection can be treated as a image segmentation task. Zhang et al. [19] made use of FCN for multi-oriented text detection. EAST [20] devised a deep FCN-based pipeline that directly completed the word or line level prediction.

Our work is mainly inspired by recent work [1]. Similar to SSD, we utilize multiple feature layers for text detection. We introduce Text Detection Layers and two improved strategies for better long text line detection. Also, we present a Text Verification Model based on encoder-decoder network, experiments show that recognitions of initial detection results can help refine final results of text detection.

3 Methodology

In this section, we will present our network structure and details of proposed method. The key component of the proposed method is Text Localization Neural Network for initial text detection, also, Text Verification Model is proposed for eliminating incorrectly localized text regions.

3.1 Text Localization Neural Network

Network Design. Structure of our Text Localization Neural Network is illustrated in Fig. 2. The proposed network is a 28-layer fully convolutional network including two parts, one part is a 13-layer base network keeping conv_1 to conv5_3 in VGG-16 [21], and the last two fully connected layers in VGG-16 are replaced with conv6 and conv7 respectively in Fig. 2. The other part are 15 extra layers, including 9 extra convolutional layers and 6 Text Detection Layers.

Text Detection Layers. Similar to original SSD model, Text Detection Layers make use of multiple feature maps for prediction. In every location of a feature map cell, Text Detection Layers output offsets of a default text bounding box to its matched ground truth boxes. Also, Text Detection Layers are able to output text/non-text confidence of the corresponding area. Text Detection Layers output a 6 dimensional vector for a default text bounding box.

Larger Aspect Ratios. As in [1], to handle different object scales, SSD imposes different aspect ratios for the default boxes, and denotes them as $a_r = \{1, 2, 3, \frac{1}{2}, \frac{1}{3}\}$. However, different from the general object, the horizontal scene text especially Chinese text, tends to have more scales with larger aspect ratios. Therefore, we retain 3 aspect rations (1, 2, 3) of the original a_r, and also define 4 more aspect rations (5, 7, 9, 10) which obtained from the experiment, i.e. $a_r = \{1, 2, 3, 5, 7, 9, 10\}$. In each location of a feature map cell, our Text Localization Neural Network produces text/non-text presence confidence and four offsets, resulting in a 84-d vector. Larger aspect ratio of our default text bounding boxes are illustrated in Fig. 3.

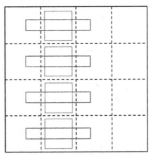

Fig. 3. Examples of default text bounding boxes in a 4 × 4 feature map cell. Default boxes locate at the center of a feature map cell. Note that for simplicity, only aspect ratios 1 and 7 are plotted.

Default Boxes with Vertical Offsets. In case of some dense text areas in natural scene images, we make offsets to default text bounding boxes in feature map cell. We make offsets about half of the height of each feature map cell in vertical direction, and more ground truth text boxes can be matched by producing more default text bounding boxes via this simple improvement. The effectiveness of vertical offsets is depicted in Fig. 4.

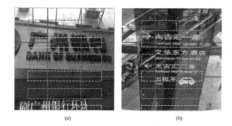

Fig. 4. Vertical offsets of default text bounding boxes on 3 × 3 feature map cell. Through vertical offsets, yellow text bounding boxes can be produced, and more text areas are able to be covered. (Color figure online)

Loss Function. Our loss function for initial text detection uses the form of multi-task loss [1], which is defined as:

$$L(x, c, l, g) = \frac{1}{N} (L_{conf}(x, c) + \alpha L_{loc}(x, l, g)) \tag{1}$$

where N is matched numbers of default text bounding boxes to ground-truth boxes, α is the weight term, x marks whether a default text bounding box i matches a ground-truth box j. L_{conf} is 2-softmax loss produced by classifying text/non-text regions. L_{loc} is regression loss generated by a default box regressing to corresponding ground-truth boxes.

3.2 Text Verification Model

Overview. We proposed Text Verification Model to eliminate incorrect initial detection results. Our text verification model is based on encoder-decoder network, which further makes use of text recognition results to refine detection.

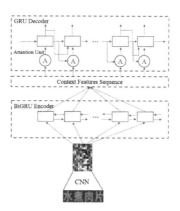

Fig. 5. Architecture of Text Verification Model. The model is composed of encoder network and decoder network.

Architecture of Text Verification Model is depicted in Fig. 5. The encoder network is composed of CNN and BiGRU network, therefore text image features with rich context information can be encoded. The decoder network makes use of encoded features to perform recognition, therefore non-text regions can be eliminated.

Encoder Network. Our encoder network is composed of CNN Model and BiGRU network. A CNN model is used to extract image features. To better learn the dependencies and relationships between characters in input image, we then apply BiGRU to encode these features. The input image has a size of 100×32, we then adopt the same CNN architecture as in Convolution Recurrent Neural Network (CRNN) [22] to acquire a feature sequence of length 25. The hidden unit has a size of 512 in BiGRU, therefore the encoded feature sequence includes 25 feature vectors of size 1024.

Decoder Network. We adopt GRU network with attention mechanism [23] to decode the sequential features into words.

Firstly, encode features at all steps from the output of encoder BiGRU are fed into decoder GRU. As for decoder GRU, the ground-truth word label is adopted as input during training. At each time step, we use the same attention function as in [24] to make decoder GRU more focused on current input. Output space takes 3775 common Chinese characters into account, also '#' character is used for background regions, and a special END token is used. That's to say, output space has a size of 3777. At test time, the token with the highest probability in previous output is selected as the input token at next step.

4 Experiments

In this paper, our proposed method focuses on the horizontal scene text especially Chinese text. Therefore, the datasets such as ICDAR 2003, ICDAR 2013 and SVT, which mainly contain images with English texts, are not applicable for our experiment. In this section, we evaluate the proposed method on our text detection dataset, which is composed of the scene images by mobile phone shooting and some horizontal scene text images in RCTW 2017 (ICDAR 2017 Competition on Read Chinese Text in the Wild), containing 9k training images and 3k test images. The evaluation protocol are Precision, Recall and F-Measure.

4.1 Effectiveness of Text Localization Neural Network

To perform initial text detection in a fast and elegant way, we design Text Detection Layers based on SSD model, which are able to predict text in single forward pass and a standard non-maximum suppression. Besides, we add larger aspect ratios for default text bounding boxes and make vertical offsets of them to better cover scene text in images.

Fig. 6. Qualitative results of Text Localization Neural Network on our dataset. Green solid boxes are detected scene text. Red dashed boxes are ignored scene text. (Color figure online)

Comparison with SSD. Table 1 compares results of our Text Localization Neural Network and SSD. In terms of precision, recall and F-Measure, Text Localization Neural Network outperforms SSD by a large margin.

Table 1. Performance comparisons with SSD

Model	Precision	Recall	F-Measure
SSD	75.9	56.8	65.0
Text Localization Neural Network	**80.5**	**78.4**	**79.4**

Example Results. Figure 6 shows some qualitative results on our dataset. As can be seen, Text Localization Neural Network can handle horizontal scene text especially dense and long text well.

4.2 Effectiveness of Text Verification Model

Table 2 shows evaluation results after adopting Text Verification Model. After eliminating False Positive (FP) detections, our detection precision raises by 3.1%.

Table 2. Performance comparisons after applying Text Verification Model

Model	Precision	Recall	F-Measure
Text Localization Neural Network	80.5	78.4	79.4
Text Localization Neural Network + Text Verification Model	**83.0**	78.4	**80.6**

4.3 Comparison with Other Methods

Table 3 lists and compares the results of the proposed method and other state-of-the-art methods. As we can see, our method achieves the highest recall rate of 0.784, while only slightly lower in precision than CTPN [16]. Overall, our proposed method in scene text detection has a good performance.

Table 3. Performance comparisons with some of the state-of-the-art methods

Method	Precision	Recall	F-Measure
CNN + MSERS (Huang et al. [13])	80.7	67.9	73.7
CTPN (Tian et al. [16])	**84.3**	77.8	**80.9**
Multi-oriented FCN (Zhang et al. [19])	80.7	74.6	77.5
FCRN (Gupta et al. [18])	82.9	72.2	77.2
Our method	83.0	**78.4**	80.6

5 Conclusion

We have presented an effective method for natural scene text detection based on SSD and encoder-decoder network. We make improvement on SSD to better handle horizontal text detection, especially long text in natural scenes. We also proposed an encoder-decoder network and make use of recognition results to refine detection results. Comprehensive evaluations and results on our constructed dataset well demonstrate the effectiveness of our proposed method.

For future works, one potential direction is extending the proposed model considering the deformation of text to handle multi-oriented texts from the pixel level. Furthermore, scene texts with multiple orientations, fonts and colors can be better detected.

Acknowledgments. This research was partially supported by National science and technology support plan (2013BAH65F04), Natural Science Foundation of Guangdong Province (No. 2015A030313210) and Science and Technology Program of Guangzhou (Grant No.: 201604010061, 201707010141).

References

1. Liu, W., et al.: SSD: single shot MultiBox detector. In: Leibe, B., Matas, J., Sebe, N., Welling, M. (eds.) ECCV 2016. LNCS, vol. 9905, pp. 21–37. Springer, Cham (2016). https://doi.org/10.1007/978-3-319-46448-0_2
2. Shi, B., et al.: ICDAR2017 competition on reading Chinese text in the wild (RCTW-17) (2017)
3. Kim, K.I., Jung, K., Kim, J.H.: Texture-based approach for text detection in images using support vector machines and continuously adaptive mean shift algorithm. IEEE Trans. Pattern Anal. Mach. Intell. **25**, 1631–1639 (2003)
4. Phan, T.Q., Shivakumara, P., Tan, C.L.: A Laplacian method for video text detection. In: 10th International Conference on Document Analysis and Recognition, ICDAR 2009, pp. 66–70 (2009)
5. Wang, K., Belongie, S.: Word spotting in the wild. In: Daniilidis, K., Maragos, P., Paragios, N. (eds.) ECCV 2010. LNCS, vol. 6311, pp. 591–604. Springer, Heidelberg (2010). https://doi.org/10.1007/978-3-642-15549-9_43
6. Epshtein, B., Ofek, E., Wexler, Y.: Detecting text in natural scenes with stroke width transform. In: Computer Vision and Pattern Recognition, CVPR, pp. 2963–2970 (2010)
7. Chowdhury, A.R., Bhattacharya, U., Parui, S.K.: Scene text detection using sparse stroke information and MLP. In: 21st International Conference on Pattern Recognition, ICPR, pp. 294–297 (2012)
8. Yao, C., Bai, X., Liu, W., Ma, Y., Tu, Z.: Detecting texts of arbitrary orientations in natural images. In: IEEE Conference on Computer Vision and Pattern Recognition, CVPR, pp. 1083–1090 (2012)
9. Matas, J., Chum, O., Urban, M., Pajdla, T.: Robust wide-baseline stereo from maximally stable extremal regions. Image Vis. Comput. **22**, 761–767 (2004)
10. Shahab, A., Shafait, F., Dengel, A.: Robust reading competition challenge 2: reading text in scene images. In: IEEE International Conference on Document Analysis and Recognition, pp. 1491–1496 (2011)
11. Karatzas, D., et al.: ICDAR 2013 robust reading competition. In: IEEE International Conference on Document Analysis and Recognition, pp. 1484–1493 (2013)
12. Sun, L., Huo, Q., Jia, W., Chen, K.: Robust text detection in natural scene images by generalized color-enhanced contrasting extremal region and neural networks. In: IEEE 22nd International Conference on Pattern Recognition, ICPR, pp. 2715–2720 (2014)
13. Huang, W., Qiao, Y., Tang, X.: Robust scene text detection with convolution neural network induced MSER trees. In: Fleet, D., Pajdla, T., Schiele, B., Tuytelaars, T. (eds.) ECCV 2014. LNCS, vol. 8692, pp. 497–511. Springer, Cham (2014). https://doi.org/10.1007/978-3-319-10593-2_33
14. Ren, S., He, K., Girshick, R., Sun, J.: Faster R-CNN: towards real-time object detection with region proposal networks. IEEE Trans. Pattern Anal. Mach. Intell. **39**, 1137–1149 (2017)
15. Zhong, Z., Jin, L., Zhang, S., Feng, Z.: DeepText: a unified framework for text proposal generation and text detection in natural images, pp. 1–18. arXiv preprint arXiv:1605.07314 (2015)
16. Tian, Z., Huang, W., He, T., He, P., Qiao, Y.: Detecting text in natural image with connectionist text proposal network. In: Leibe, B., Matas, J., Sebe, N., Welling, M. (eds.) ECCV 2016. LNCS, vol. 9912, pp. 56–72. Springer, Cham (2016). https://doi.org/10.1007/978-3-319-46484-8_4

17. Redmon, J., Divvala, S., Girshick, R., Farhadi, A.: You only look once: unified, real-time object detection. In: Computer Vision and Pattern Recognition, pp. 779–788 (2016)
18. Gupta, A., Vedaldi, A., Zisserman, A.: Synthetic data for text localisation in natural images. In: Proceedings of the IEEE Conference on Computer Vision and Pattern Recognition, pp. 2315–2324 (2016)
19. Zhang, Z., Zhang, C., Shen, W., Yao, C., Liu, W., Bai, X.: Multi-oriented text detection with fully convolutional networks. In: Computer Vision and Pattern Recognition, pp. 4159–4167 (2016)
20. Zhou, X., et al.: EAST: an efficient and accurate scene text detector, pp. 2642–2651 (2017)
21. Simonyan, K., Zisserman, A.: Very deep convolutional networks for large-scale image recognition. Computer Science (2014)
22. Shi, B., Bai, X., Yao, C.: An end-to-end trainable neural network for image-based sequence recognition and its application to scene text recognition. IEEE Trans. Pattern Anal. Mach. Intell. **39**, 2298–2304 (2017)
23. Luong, M.T., Pham, H., Manning, C.D.: Effective approaches to attention-based neural machine translation. Computer Science (2015)
24. Bahdanau, D., Cho, K., Bengio, Y.: Neural machine translation by jointly learning to align and translate. Computer Science (2014)

Effective SVD-Based Deep Network Compression for Automatic Speech Recognition

Hao Fu[1]([✉])[iD], Yue Ming[1], Yibo Jiang[2], and Chunxiao Fan[1]

[1] Beijing University of Posts and Telecommunications, Beijing, China
{fuhao2013,yming,eetxwl}@bupt.edu.cn
[2] Ningbo Xitang Technologies Inc., Ningbo, China
jiangybtt@163.com

Abstract. Neural networks improve speech recognition performance significantly, but their large amount of parameters brings high computation and memory cost. To work around this problem, we propose an efficient network compression method based on Singular Value Decomposition (SVD), Simultaneous Iterative SVD Reconstruction via Loss Sensitive Update (SISVD-LU). Firstly, we analyse the matrices' singular values to learn the sparsity in every single layer and then we apply SVD on the most sparse layer to factorize the weight matrix into two or more matrices with least reconstruction errors. Secondly, we reconstruct the model using our *Loss Sensitive Update* strategy, which propagates the error across layers. Finally, we utilize *Simultaneous Iterative Compression* method, which factorizes all layers simultaneously and then iteratively minimize the model size while keeping the accuracy. We evaluate the proposed approach on the two different LVCSR datasets, AISHELL and TIMIT. On AISHELL mandarin dataset, we can obtain 50% compression ratio in single layer while maintaining almost the same accuracy. When introducing update, our simultaneous iterative compression can further boost the compression ratio, finally reduce model size by 43%. Similar experimental results are also obtained on TIMIT. Both results are gained with slight accuracy loss.

Keywords: Speech recognition · SVD-based compression ·
Loss sensitive update · Simultaneous iteration

1 Introduction

In the past few years, we have witnessed a rapid development of deep neural networks in the field of automatic speech recognition (ASR) [8,14,18,21,22]. However, the large size of neural network models leads to high computation and memory costs, which also makes it difficult to deploy the models in low resource devices. Frequently-used solution is to put the models on powerful cloud servers. But when network-connection is instable, this approach brings high latency, and

© Springer Nature Switzerland AG 2019
X. Bai et al. (Eds.): FFER 2018/DLPR 2018, LNCS 11264, pp. 35–47, 2019.
https://doi.org/10.1007/978-3-030-12177-8_4

even failure. Thus, neural networks compression for mobile devices attracts more and more attention.

Recent researches have proposed various methods to compress models, which can be efficiently executed directly on the embedded devices. Existing methods for neural network compression can be broadly divided into four categories: parameter quantization, pruning, knowledge distillation and low rank approximation.

Parameter quantization attempts to quantize the weights or activations of networks from 32 bit floating point into lower bit-width representations. With just two-three bits per parameter, these methods can get pretty good compression performance [6,12,15,23]. However it requires the algorithm computationally efficient while reducing runtime memory footprint.

Pruning is a forthright way to reduce network complexity. [11] pioneered the approach of pruning. They trained a full network and removed the neurons with the zero activations. The work in [20] exploited the sparseness in DNN, and presented a nice way to reduce the model size. [4] jointly learned weights and connections, using a hard threshold to remove the least important weights with small absolute values. Finally, they then fine-tuned to recover its accuracy. It has successfully pruned the heavy networks without performance loss. But it still need extra memory usage to index the non-zero value.

Knowledge distillation method first trains a heavier network, as "teacher" network, then trains a smaller "student" network through knowledge transfer. First attempts in this direction were made by [2], they investigated the model complexity- RMSE error. [5] then utilized the predicted probability distribution of the teacher model as "knowledge", introducing a more general technique for distilling the knowledge of a network.

Low-rank approximation is also widely studied [3,17,19]. In recent years, low-rank tensor approximation methods, e.g. Singular Value Decomposition (SVD), have been established as a new tool in matrix compression to address large-scale parameters problem. Reducing parameter dimensions by low-rank approximation saves storage and reduces time complexity simultaneously.

Our work builds on previous research in the area of low rank decomposition, called ***Simultaneous Iterative SVD Reconstruction via Loss Sensitive Update*** (**SISVD-LU**). Initially, a large model trained without constraints is produced. We conduct the first phase of our method to learn the importance of each weight matrix in different layers. We keep the essential information remained (indicated by larger singular values), and surpress less useful ones. Then, we update the reconstructed network in a optimal procedure so that the removed information can be compensated. In the end, reconstruction and update are iteratively performed to further reduce network complexity and keep the accuracy at a acceptable level.

Our work is different from the previous works in follow aspects:

1. Most methods [3,7,19] approximate a tensor by minimizing the reconstruction error of the original parameters, while ignoring the accumulate errors. Our update mechanism emphasizes the ultimate network objective goal by

applying across-layer loss sensitive update. Furthermore, we iterate the process which is different from their methods.

2. Compared with [13], we compress the Time Delay Neural Network (TDNN) for ASR instead of Convolutional Neural Network (CNN). We also aware the importance of global loss, but we further explore the case of single-layer compression, and propose our exclusive update.

3. Prior approaches are usually evaluated on over-parameterized models, such as AlexNet [10], VGG [16], or very large output full-connection layers. Our method can get about 50% compression rate while only applied in the relatively small hidden layers.

The rest of this paper is organized as follows. Section 2 details every phase of our proposed method. Experimental results are presented and discussed in Sect. 3. In Sect. 4, we summarize our work.

2   Effective SVD-Based Deep Network Compression

Our proposed method, called Simultaneous Iterative SVD Reconstruction via Loss Sensitive Update (SISVD-LU), including three phases:

2.1   Inner-Layer Reconstruction Using SVD

In our proposed method, a full-trained deep neural network model is firstly obtained without resource constraints. Then, we decompose the weights matrix $W^{(l)}$ between the l-th and $(l+1)$-th layers via matrix factorization (MF) to reduce the parameter size.

We formulate *the Matrix Approximation* problem as follow.

$$W = \hat{W} + \varepsilon \qquad (1)$$

as Eq. 1 shows, the weight matrix W is subject to the *Additive-Residual* model. Where the weight matrix $W^{(l)}$ is generalized as $W \ (\in \mathbb{R}^{M \times N})$ with rank r, $\varepsilon \in \mathbb{R}^{M \times N}$ is the reconstructed residual matrix. And $\hat{W}$ is the approximate low-rank matrix. We can view this procedure as capturing the main patterns of W while eliminating much of "noise".

We use Singular Value Decomposition (SVD) to solve this rank minimization problem. The matrix $W^{(l)}$ has a representation of the form:

$$W^{(l)} = U \Sigma_r V^{\mathsf{T}} \qquad (2)$$

where U and V are orthogonal matrices $UU^T = VV^T = I$, and Σ_r is a diagonal matrix, $\Sigma_r = diag(\sigma_1, \sigma_2, ..., \sigma_r)$, are called *singular values*. The size of the original matrix $W^{(l)}$ is $M \times r$. The resulting decomposition submatrix U, Σ_r, V size $M \times r$, $r \times r$, $r \times N$, respectively. Here r denotes the number of the nonzero singular values.

It is found that the singular value decreases particularly fast. In many cases, the sum of top 10% of singular values accounts for more than 99% of the sum of all singular values [19]. For compression task, a small preserved rank k will be chosen. We sort singular values in a descending order and pick the largest k ($k \ll r$) singular vectors in U and V with corresponding eigenvalue in Σ to approximate W.

$$\hat{W} = \hat{U}\hat{\Sigma}_k\hat{V}^\top$$
$$= \hat{U}\hat{\Sigma}^{\frac{1}{2}} \cdot (\hat{V}\hat{\Sigma}^{\frac{1}{2}})^\top \tag{3}$$

The approximation of SVD is controlled by the decay along the eigenvalues in Σ_k. This procedure changes the number of parameters from $M \times N$ to $k \times (M + N)$. So the *Compression Ratio* $\mathcal{R}$ is defined as $\mathcal{R} = \dfrac{k \times (M + N)}{M \times N}$.
The demonstration of SVD is presented in the right part of Fig. 1.

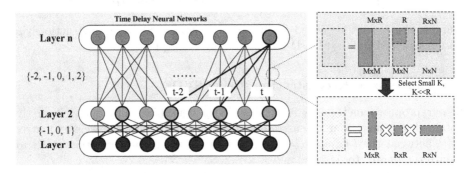

Fig. 1. Architecture of SVD-based network reconstruction. Left part is the baseline TDNN model structure, right part illustrates the process of SVD.

2.2 Across-Layer Loss Sensitive Update

From a across-layer perspective, the inner-layer decomposition causes cumulative errors and destroys the coupling of the layers. We build the *Loss-sensitive Update* recipe.

In a vanilla neural network, the input features are presented as $X = [x_1, x_2, ..., x_m]$, where $x_i \in \mathbb{R}^d$, where m is the number of feature vectors and d is dimension of a feature vector. After forward propagation, the output of the l-th layer can be written as:

$$y_i^{(l)} = \sigma(z_i^{(l)}), \; where \; z_i^{(l)} = \sum_{j=1}^{n^{(l-1)}} w_{ij}^{(l-1)} x_j^{(l-1)} \tag{4}$$

Where $w_{ij}^{(l-1)}$ is the element of weight matrix $W^{(l-1)}$. $n^{(l-1)}$ denotes the number of neurons in the $l-1$ layer. And $\sigma(\cdot)$ is a non-linear transformation called "activation function". The commonly used forms of this function are: tanh, sigmoid or the rectifier linear unit (ReLU) etc. The hidden state and its result after activation are denoted as vectors $z_i^{(l)}$ and $y_i^{(l)}$, respectively. Expanding the expression to Eq. 5.

$$y_i^{(l)} = \sigma(w^{(l-1)} \cdots \sigma(w^{(2)}\sigma(w^{(1)}x^{(1)} + b^{(1)}) + b^{(2)}) \cdots + b^{(l-1)}) \tag{5}$$

We can see more clearly how the global error accumulated after decomposition. Most existing reconstruction focus on how to reduce the error of inner-layer reconstruction, as showed in Eq. 6. Here $||\cdot||_F$ as Frobenius norm. In this way, the loss of global accuracy is often ignored.

$$\mathcal{C}_1 = \min_{\hat{W}^{(l)}} \frac{1}{2} \left\| W^{(l)} - \hat{W}^{(l)} \right\|_F^2 \tag{6}$$

Single-layer reconstruction weakens the strong associations between layers, which are built through forward and backward propagation. Hence, we solve the reconstruction problem for a broader scope, aiming at preserving the global modeling capabilities of networks, such as classification ability or regression ability. Our loss function is modeled as Eq. 7.

$$\begin{aligned}
\mathcal{C}_2 &= \min_{\hat{W}^{(l-1)}} \frac{1}{2} \left\| Y^{(l)} - \sigma(\hat{W}^{(l-1)}X) \right\|_F^2 \\
&= \min_{\hat{w}_{ij}^{(l-1)}} \sum_{i=1}^{n^{(l)}} \sum_{j=1}^{n^{(l-1)}} \frac{1}{2} \left\| y_i^{(l)} - \sigma(\hat{w}_{ij}^{(l-1)}x_j) \right\|_2^2
\end{aligned} \tag{7}$$

In order to further constrain the complexity of the model, we add the L1-regularization term to the objective function, inducing model to be sparse. Our final objective function is Eq. 8.

$$\mathcal{L} = \min_{\hat{W}^{(l-1)}} \frac{1}{2} \left\| Y^{(l)} - \sigma(\hat{W}^{(l-1)}X) \right\|_F^2 + \Psi_\lambda(\hat{W})$$

$$s.t. \quad \Psi_\lambda(\hat{W}) = \lambda \sum_{i=1}^{n^{(l)}} \sum_{j=1}^{n^{(l-1)}} ||\hat{w}_{ij}||_1 \tag{8}$$

Then we backpropagate loss using *Stochastic Gradient Descent* (SGD). Note that SVD will insert a bottleneck layer in the middle of the original layer. In backpropagation phase, we keep the structure.

According to the different scopes of global loss backpropagation, we propose the following methods:

- **Scheme 1** Fix the decomposition layers, only update the remaining layers, we call it *Exclusive Update*.

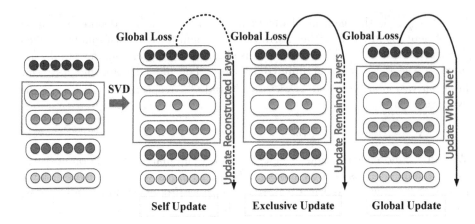

Fig. 2. Different update schemes of global loss backpropagation. Here, the rounded rectangle represents a hidden layer, and the circle represents neuron. The dashed line indicates that backpropagation does not change the parameters of the specific layers, and the solid line indicates that backpropagation will update the parameters those layers.

- **Scheme 2** Only update decomposition layers, keep the remaining layers unchanged, we call it *Self Update*.
- **Scheme 3** Update the whole reconstructed model, we call it *Global Update*.

The range of error back-propagation is controlled by the learning rate of each layer. If the learning rate is set to zero, this layer parameter is not updated. Demonstration of different global loss backpropagation schemes is presented in Fig. 2.

2.3   Iterative Compression

As previous section summarized, across-layer reconstruction can utilize SVD-based compression performance to make the neural networks small and fast enough. Based on the above analysis, we find that iteratively apply inner-layer decomposition and across-layer reconstruction procedure will bring high compression ratio with low accuracy loss. We perform the iterative compression in two different ways:

- *Layerwise Compression*: Conduct network reconstruction after compression of single layer during every iteration.
- *Simultaneous Compression*: Compress the whole networks at same time, and fine-tuning follows iteratively.

The back-propagation of the cumulative errors can retrieve the discriminal ability damage of models and preserve original relationships across the networks. Our proposed method reduces network complexity and keep the accuracy in a acceptable level. Figure 3 describes two iterative compression flows.

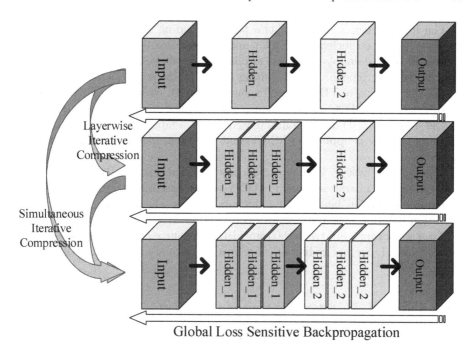

Global Loss Sensitive Backpropagation

Fig. 3. Two iterative compression approaches: simultaneous compression, layerwise compression. Layerwise compression will get the bottom state from top step by step. Simultaneous compression will go to the bottom state directly. Here, the cube represents the weight matrix, it is decomposed into three smaller matrices by SVD.

3 Experiments

In this section, we evaluate the effectiveness of our approach on two different LVCSR corpus, AISHELL [1] for Mandarin ASR and TIMIT for English ASR.

3.1 Experimental Setup

Architecture of TDNN. Since speech signal has the temporal dynamics property, an acoustic model is required to have the ability to capture the long term dependencies between acoustic events. In a standard DNN, the initial layer learns the entire temporal context. Whereas, the TDNN architecture learns in a hierarchical structure. Narrow contexts are learnt by low layers and the deeper, layers learn from a wider temporal context. Hence the higher layers have the ability to learn wider temporal relationships. The structure of TDNN is depicted in the left part of Fig. 1.

3.2 Mandarin LVCSR Task on AISHELL

AISHELL corpus is a 170-h Mandarin speech corpus [1]. The corpus includes training set (150 h), development set (10 h) and test sets (5 h).

The input features consist of two parts, including 13-dimensional Mel frequency cepstral coefficients (MFCC) and 3-dimensional pitch features. Mean normalization and double deltas are applied on the above features before feeding into the training pipeline. The resulting GMM-HMM model has 2952 senones. During the training of TDNN-based acoustic models, we input high resolutional (40-dimensional) MFCC and 3-dimensional pitch features. Audio augmentation [9] and i-Vector (100-dimensional) based DNN adaptation are applied. Subsampling window is applied on MFCC and pitch features to splice neighboring frames.

Our baseline system is constructed based on the corresponding recipe. We used time delay neural network (TDNN) as our baseline. In our experiments, it contains 6 hidden layers, 850 hidden nodes per layer, using ReLU as the activation function. The output layer consisted of 2952 units.

After we obtain a full-trained (train with no resource constraints) deep neural network model, further reduction of footprint is conducted by an SVD-based compression.

Rank Selection. We notice that rank selection affects the compression rate as well as the accuracy. Too high rank will result in insufficient compression, while too low may make the accuracy recovery difficult or impossible.

To explore the implicit information each layer contains, we apply SVD on the same layer with different ranks, and different layers with the same rank.

Tables 1 and 2 summarizes the experimental results. The first column describes the setup of the model, and the number in bracket means that how many singular values we keep after SVD. The third column is the number of parameters in each model. For example, in the original DNN model the number of parameters is $315 \times 850 + (850 \times 850) \times 6 + 850 \times 2952 \approx 6.78M$. Baseline GMM model has $100K$ gaussians in total.

Table 1. Results for SVD reconstruction **on the same single layer** preserving **different ranks** in AISHELL task (without fine-tune). Numbers inside brackets represent the preserved singular values. The digits in the table represent the **word error rate** (WER) (%). NoP denotes number of parameters

Acoustic model	test	dev	NoP
6th(128)	10.08	8.33	0.21M
6th(256)	8.62	7.4	0.42M
6th(512)	8.49	7.28	0.83M

From Table 1, we can see that model size of our original DNN model is nearly twice as GMM model. We reduce WER at 30% relatively by replacing GMM model with DNN model. Using different preserved ranks in the same layer lead to a nonlinear loss of precision.

Table 2. Results for SVD reconstruction **on different layers** preserving **the same rank** in AISHELL task (without fine-tune)

Acoustic model	test	dev	Prior NoP	Post NoP
GMM	12.10	10.40	- - -	- - -
TDNN	8.45	7.20	6.78M	- - -
2nd hidden layer(256)	9.99	8.47	0.68M	0.41M
3rd hidden layer(256)	8.87	7.62	0.68M	0.41M
4th hidden layer(256)	8.97	7.6	0.68M	0.41M
5th hidden layer(256)	8.67	7.42	0.68M	0.41M
6th hidden layer(256)	**8.62**	**7.4**	**0.68M**	**0.41M**
Output layer(256)	14.01	13.84	2.39M	0.92M
All hidden layers(256)	**22.12**	**19.58**	**6.78M**	**3.89M**

The following rows in Table 2 reveal the effect of the proposed approach. When we keep only top 50% singular values (the SVD-256 case) on the matrices of hidden layers, there are slight changes compared with original model. But when it comes to compress the output layer, keep top 50% singular values will cause obvious performance reduction. Therefore, different scaled weight matrices should keep different ranks.

As it were, SVD in the most sparse layer can effectively compress model size, even without reconstruction update. We can at most gain 50% compression ratio after applying SVD, while maintaining almost the same accuracy.

Across-Layer Loss Sensitive Update. We conduct several experiments, the results are described in Table 3. For single layer decomposition, the *Self Update* scheme and the *Global Update* scheme both work good for single-layer (or a small amount of layers). For multi-layer decomposition, *Global Update* scheme shows more advantages. Furthermore, we explore if train for more epochs, the *Self Update* can get better results. But it leads to a painful long time consumption, and doesn't look better than *Global Update* case (result: WER on dev set is 7.35%, on test set is 8.61%, re-train for 3 epoch,).

We believe that it is owing that the cumulative losses from SVD can affect the entire network, *Global Update* is more reasonable to give reconstructed model a larger adjustable range. On the other hand, since SVD maintains the principal components of the original weight matrix, we can take it for a pre-training procedure.

As a periodic summary, *Global Update* is suitable for more scenarios.

Iterative Compression. We perform experiments to compare our two iterative compression methods. Here "Aggressive" means directly push model to a relatively small size and Global Update repeatedly. "Gradual" mode means

Table 3. Comparisons of different update schemes after weight matrices reconstruction in AISHELL task

Acoustic model	Fine-tune Scheme	WER	
		test	dev
TDNN, Baseline	- - -	8.45	7.20
6th Hidden Layer(256)	Exclusive Update	8.59	7.36
	Self Update	**8.49**	**7.31**
	Global Update	8.55	7.36
All Hidden Layers(256)	Exclusive Update	9.45	8.08
	Self Update	8.37	7.22
	Global Update	**8.33**	**7.14**

compress to a moderate size first and iterative push to a smaller size, fine-tune is executed after every iteration. Table 4 shows our comparison results.

Table 4. Comparisons of different iterative compression schemes for combination of reconstruction and update in AISHELL task

Iterative scheme	Mode	test	dev
Layerwise compression	**Input to Output**	**8.59**	**7.36**
	Output to Input	8.63	7.41
Simultaneous compression	**Aggressive(850-128)**	**8.49**	**7.31**
	Gradual(850-512-256-128)	8.55	7.36

From the exhibited results, we found that the *Simultaneous Compression* looks better than *Layerwise Compression*. Moreover, proceeding from input to output rather that the reverse order produces better results for layerwise compression. "Agressive" mode for Simultaneous compression shows more effectiveness.

Results. Here we summarize the best result on AISHELL in Table 5 with SISVD-LU.

We get the best result when we factorize all hidden layers with rank 256 and iterative global update. The parameter size of the final compressed model is $315 \times 850 + (850 \times 128 + 128 \times 850) \times 6 + 850 \times 2952 \approx 3.89M$, which is 57% of the original size.

3.3   English LVCSR Task on TIMIT

We demonstrate scalability of the proposed low-rank decomposition on a different dataset. So our second task is to train a same-structure TDNN model for English ASR corpus TIMIT to verify our conclusion is universal.

Table 5. Experimental results on the Mandarin AISHELL Corpus using our SISVD-GLU approach

Acoustic model		test	dev
TDNN, Baseline	- - -	8.45	7.20
All Hidden Layers(512)	Before Iterative Update	8.54	7.32
	After Iterative Update	8.42	7.21
All Hidden Layers(256)	Before Iterative Update	22.12	19.58
	After Iterative Update	**8.32**	**7.12**
All Hidden Layers(128)	Before Iterative Update	34.55	30.71
	After Iterative Update	8.49	7.31

The two corpora are significantly different in language and duration. TIMIT contains a total of 6300 sentences (5.4 h), consisting of 10 sentences spoken by each of 630 speakers from 8 major dialect regions of the United States.

In our experiments, we use 13 dimensional features space maximum likelihood linear regression (fMLLR) features and then concatenate the neighboring 5 frames (11 frames in total) as the input feature. Note that, we don't use i-Vector in following experiments. To have a fair comparison, we construct a same TDNN architecture (number of hidden units and number of layers are the same) as the one used on last task.

We first train a full-trained model and then perform SISVD-LU. Table 6 shows us the results.

Table 6. Experimental results on the English TIMIT corpus using our SISVD-GLU approach

Acoustic model		test	dev
TDNN, Baseline	- - -	18.4	16.4
All Hidden Layers(512)	Before Iterative Update	18.7	17.4
	After Iterative Update	18.4	16.9
All Hidden Layers(256)	Before Iterative Update	23.3	21.4
	After Iterative Update	17.8	16.2
All Hidden Layers(128)	Before Iterative Update	45.2	41.5
	After Iterative Update	**17.7**	**16.1**

After compression, the accuracy after compression suffers great reduction. Yet, our iterative global update can recall the loss back. Those results fully support our method.

4   Conclusion

In this paper, we have proposed an effective SVD-based compression method. The loss sensitive update has conducted after SVD reconstruction, and repeat this combination of two operations. For the single layer, by performing our compression method, we can gain 50% compression ratio after applying SVD while maintaining almost the same accuracy. For a whole model, our iterative update procedure can boost the compression ratio, in the same time, without accuracy loss. We verify our strategies in two very different datasets, TIMIT for English ASR and AISHELL [1] for Mandarin ASR.

The experimental results support our conclusion. Though we only investigate the SVD compression method, the outcome of this paper provokes us to generalize our conclusion in other matrix manipulation related methods or combine it with other compression methods.

References

1. Bu, H., Du, J., Na, X., Wu, B., Zheng, H.: Aishell-1: An open-source mandarin speech corpus and a speech recognition baseline. arXiv preprint arXiv:1709.05522 (2017)
2. Bucilu, C., Caruana, R., Niculescu-Mizil, A.: Model compression. In: Proceedings of the 12th ACM SIGKDD International Conference on Knowledge Discovery and Data Mining, pp. 535–541. ACM (2006)
3. Denton, E.L., Zaremba, W., Bruna, J., LeCun, Y., Fergus, R.: Exploiting linear structure within convolutional networks for efficient evaluation. In: Advances in Neural Information Processing Systems, pp. 1269–1277 (2014)
4. Han, S., Pool, J., Tran, J., Dally, W.: Learning both weights and connections for efficient neural network. In: Advances in Neural Information Processing Systems, pp. 1135–1143 (2015)
5. Hinton, G., Vinyals, O., Dean, J.: Distilling the knowledge in a neural network. arXiv preprint arXiv:1503.02531 (2015)
6. Jacob, B., et al.: Quantization and training of neural networks for efficient integer-arithmetic-only inference. arXiv preprint arXiv:1712.05877 (2017)
7. Jaderberg, M., Vedaldi, A., Zisserman, A.: Speeding up convolutional neural networks with low rank expansions. arXiv preprint arXiv:1405.3866 (2014)
8. Kim, S., Hori, T., Watanabe, S.: Joint CTC-attention based end-to-end speech recognition using multi-task learning. In: 2017 IEEE International Conference on Acoustics, Speech and Signal Processing (ICASSP), pp. 4835–4839. IEEE (2017)
9. Ko, T., Peddinti, V., Povey, D., Khudanpur, S.: Audio augmentation for speech recognition. In: Sixteenth Annual Conference of the International Speech Communication Association (2015)
10. Krizhevsky, A., Sutskever, I., Hinton, G.E.: Imagenet classification with deep convolutional neural networks. In: Advances in Neural Information Processing Systems, pp. 1097–1105 (2012)
11. LeCun, Y., Denker, J.S., Solla, S.A.: Optimal brain damage. In: Advances in Neural Information Processing Systems, pp. 598–605 (1990)
12. Li, F., Zhang, B., Liu, B.: Ternary weight networks. arXiv preprint arXiv:1605.04711 (2016)

13. Lin, S., Ji, R., Guo, X., Li, X., et al.: Towards convolutional neural networks compression via global error reconstruction. In: IJCAI, pp. 1753–1759 (2016)
14. Maas, A.L., et al.: Building DNN acoustic models for large vocabulary speech recognition. Comput. Speech Lang. **41**, 195–213 (2017)
15. Rastegari, M., Ordonez, V., Redmon, J., Farhadi, A.: XNOR-Net: imagenet classification using binary convolutional neural networks. In: Leibe, B., Matas, J., Sebe, N., Welling, M. (eds.) ECCV 2016. LNCS, vol. 9908, pp. 525–542. Springer, Cham (2016). https://doi.org/10.1007/978-3-319-46493-0_32
16. Simonyan, K., Zisserman, A.: Very deep convolutional networks for large-scale image recognition. arXiv preprint arXiv:1409.1556 (2014)
17. Sindhwani, V., Sainath, T., Kumar, S.: Structured transforms for small-footprint deep learning. In: Advances in Neural Information Processing Systems, pp. 3088–3096 (2015)
18. Xiong, W., et al.: The microsoft 2016 conversational speech recognition system. In: 2017 IEEE International Conference on Acoustics, Speech and Signal Processing (ICASSP), pp. 5255–5259. IEEE (2017)
19. Xue, J., Li, J., Gong, Y.: Restructuring of deep neural network acoustic models with singular value decomposition. In: Interspeech, pp. 2365–2369 (2013)
20. Yu, D., Seide, F., Li, G., Deng, L.: Exploiting sparseness in deep neural networks for large vocabulary speech recognition. In: 2012 IEEE International Conference on Acoustics, Speech and Signal Processing (ICASSP), pp. 4409–4412. IEEE (2012)
21. Zeyer, A., Doetsch, P., Voigtlaender, P., Schlüter, R., Ney, H.: A comprehensive study of deep bidirectional LSTM RNNs for acoustic modeling in speech recognition. In: 2017 IEEE International Conference on Acoustics, Speech and Signal Processing (ICASSP), pp. 2462–2466. IEEE (2017)
22. Zhang, Y., Chan, W., Jaitly, N.: Very deep convolutional networks for end-to-end speech recognition. In: 2017 IEEE International Conference on Acoustics, Speech and Signal Processing (ICASSP), pp. 4845–4849. IEEE (2017)
23. Zhou, A., Yao, A., Guo, Y., Xu, L., Chen, Y.: Incremental network quantization: Towards lossless CNNs with low-precision weights. arXiv preprint arXiv:1702.03044 (2017)

Evaluation of Group Convolution in Lightweight Deep Networks for Object Classification

Arindam Das[1], Thomas Boulay[2], Senthil Yogamani[3(✉)], and Shiping Ou[4]

[1] Valeo, Chennai, India
arindam.das@valeo.com
[2] Valeo, Paris, France
thomas.boulay@valeo.com
[3] Valeo, Galway, Ireland
senthil.yogamani@valeo.com
[4] Valeo, Beijing, China
shiping.ou@valeo.com

Abstract. Deploying a neural network model on a low-power embedded platform is a challenging task. In this paper, we present our study on the efficacy of aggregated residual transformation (defined in ResNeXt that secured 2nd place in the ILSVRC 2016 classification task) for lightweight deep networks. The major contributions to this paper include (i) evaluation of group convolution, (ii) study on the impact of skip connection and various width for lightweight deep network. Our extensive experiments on different topologies show that employing aggregated convolution operation followed by point-wise convolution degrades the accuracy significantly. Furthermore as per our study, skip connections are not a suitable candidate for smaller networks and width is an important attribute to magnify the accuracy. Our embedded friendly networks are tested on ImageNet 2012 dataset where 3D convolution is a better alternative to aggregated convolution because of the 10% improvement in classification accuracy.

Keywords: Object classification · Convolutional Neural Network · Group convolution · Efficient networks

1 Introduction

In spite of the rapid increase in computational power of embedded systems, deploying state-of-the-art Convolution Neural Network (CNN) architectures remains to be a challenge. In some industrial applications, there are power and cost constraints which mandates smaller embedded processors. Thus it is important to design efficient models which fit the computational budget of the system. Recently, this area of research has grown significantly and there are many papers

X. Bai et al. (Eds.): FFER 2018/DLPR 2018, LNCS 11264, pp. 48–60, 2019.
https://doi.org/10.1007/978-3-030-12177-8_5

which demonstrate large improvements in runtime at a small reduction in accuracy. An overview of efficient design techniques was provided in [1] and guidelines for design of small networks is listed in [2].

Most of the research in the CNN community focus on accuracy at the cost of increased computational complexity. It is important to consider the latter as well and a multi-objective metric is necessary. A good attempt was made in [3] to compare the accuracy of networks normalized to complexity is presented. Figure 1 reproduced from this paper illustrates that there is large variability in the effective capacity of different networks. An accuracy/performance trade-off was studied in [4] for comparison of object detection meta-architectures like Faster R-CNN, R-FCN and SSD.

Group convolution is an important efficient design technique which was discussed in [1] in more detail. Although it was originally used in AlexNet in 2012, it wasn't adopted in the recent popular networks like VGG16 or ResNet. More recently, it was used in ResNeXt demonstrating a significant improvement in efficiency. This has motivated the authors to explore this design technique further in a more systematic way and provide benchmarks in particular for lighter CNN networks.

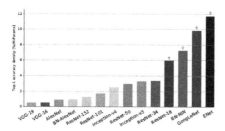

Fig. 1. Illustration of large disparity in the efficiency of networks measured by an accuracy metric normalized to number of parameters. Figure is reproduced from [3].

The rest of the paper is structured as follows. Section 1.1 provides a list of important research questions which we address in this paper with respect to grouped convolutions. Section 2 discusses related work with respect to efficient design techniques for CNN topologies. Section 3 provides implementation details of our experiments and Sect. 4 discusses the experimental results in detail. Finally, Sect. 5 summarizes the paper and provides potential future directions.

1.1 Research Questions Addressed in This Study

The effectiveness of various machine learning algorithms for vision related problems has been discussed in literature for quite a long time. Over the past few years, deep learning based techniques have received significant thrust due to their unparalleled performance. Unequivocally, one of the major application areas of such techniques is computer vision. Among various tasks under computer vision, we considered object classification as our main area of study with respect to very popular aggregated residual transformation. Our findings towards this study answer the questions below:

Does aggregated residual transformation work well for lightweight deep networks too? Well, surprisingly aggregated or group convolution fails to demonstrate its efficacy with lightweight deep networks. We witnessed that a lightweight deep network that mimicked group convolution could not outperform the same network without group convolution. The degree of this failure can be measured in terms of the difference of accuracies which is 10% as furnished in Table 1 which is non-trivial.

Do skip connections with aggregated convolution have any impact for lightweight deep networks? Interestingly we found that any lightweight deep networks comprising of skip connections with group convolution do not have much impact. Our set of experiments shown in Table 2 reveal that a lightweight deep network with skip connections outperforms the same network without skip connections by only 1% in classification task. Such small increase in accuracy does not make skip connections a reasonable candidate to be considered for embedded platform as it increases memory bandwidth.

Does drastic growth of the width in certain convolution layers have notable impact while incorporating aggregated convolution? Definitely yes. We experimented with two very lightweight residual networks where both have the same number of group convolutions but one network has incremental growth and the other one has drastic growth in number of channels. We observed a jump of more than 6% with the network having drastic growth. This is demonstrated through result in Table 3 but due to its computational cost to allow such drastic growth especially in embedded platform remains an open question to the community. To keep the computational cost affordable, the idea of drastic growth in channels can be perceived at a later stage of the network as the feature space will be comparatively less.

How does the width of the network play an influential role even without aggregated convolution and skip connection? We see significant impact in terms of accuracy as the wider network is the clear winner. We designed two very lightweight multi-layer networks where one network has double width per convolution layer in comparison to the other network. On ImageNet validation dataset, we experienced the wider network to be ahead with more than 8% margin as furnished in Table 4. Hence, the idea of having wider network can be assimilated if the objective is to classify objects aggressively with shallower networks though memory consumption and runtime should be considered with lesser priority for such case.

2   Related Work

Study on designing suitable classifiers for classification task can be found in literature dated back in 80s. Recognition of handwritten zip code [5] is one such kind of a problem. Over the time, the direction of research in the field of pattern recognition and machine learning has changed exceptionally. Few years ago, feature engineering approach where handcrafted features such as SIFT [6], HOG [7] were believed to be the best discriminative representation were used with machine learning classifiers. Later, researchers found an absolutely different dimension that is network engineering to outperform the performance of classical machine learning techniques. Thus deep learning came into the scene.

It became very easy to learn large invariant features from large-scale dataset such as ImageNet [8] that consists of 1000 classes of total 1.28 million training images. Krizhevsky et al. presented a convolutional neural network that was distributed over two GPUs as the hardware resource was limited. Performing convolution in distributed fashion has now become popular to mimic not due to hardware limitation but to amplify the accuracy along with reduced model size. Lin et al. [9] furnished "Network-in-Network" concept where a single neuron was modified to act as an independent network. VGG-nets [10] is the first very deep neural network that showed its encouraging performance. This architecture is basically comprising of many convolutional layers that are stacked one after another of same shape. VGG-16 and VGG-19 are mainly two variants of VGG-nets. The idea to construct a deeper network with repetitive blocks of same size was perceived in ResNet [11]. He et al. also presented the notion of skip connection in the same network. This kind of approach has been proved to be robust. Many variants of ResNet are available and often seen to be customized as task specific.

Xie et al. [12] inherited the concept of residual block and introduced aggregated residual transformation within each block. This transformation is also known as group convolution. Instead of performing 3D convolution over many number of channels together, it is better to perform same convolution operation with limited number of channels in parallel and later do point-wise convolution to blend the features across channels. This approach has been exhibited to be reasonably cost effective and helpful to magnify the performance of ResNet. Inception network [13] is another approach to bring down the computational cost with large margin. The core idea of inception network is to conduct convolution operation with different set of kernel size on same set of features and concatenate all the feature maps to the next layer. Due to the presence of multiple kernel size within the same layer, this network is able to capture features of all categories from each inception module and this technique can be imbibed within the residual block as well.

Though above discussed deep networks perform unarguably well but lately some research in parallel on a different dimension started with convolutional neural network. Basically how these fancy features can be accommodated on embedded platform. SqueezeNet [14] is definitely one among many such attempts that brought down the number of hyperparameters and model size ridiculously. ShuffleNet [15] is another notable effort that made the deep neural network to become lightweight for handheld devices. Our present study is concentrated to evaluate the influence of recent commonly used features for lightweight network.

3   Implementation Details

Our models are implemented using publicly Caffe framework [16] developed by Berkeley AI Research (BAIR)/The Berkeley Vision and Learning Center (BVLC). Our training strategy mostly follows [12]. ImageNet 2012 dataset [8] has been used to train and test our models. In order to do scale augmentation, each image is randomly sampled as 256×256 using its shorter stride. Resized images are further randomly cropped as 224×224 along with its horizontal flip into consideration. No other pre-processing is performed except per pixel based mean subtraction as mentioned in [8] on the extracted patches. We reduced the problem space at various convolutions layers using sub-sampling or pooling layer. This helped to reduce the number of hyper-parameters significantly. Batch normalization [17] is adopted at each layer after performing convolution operation and before using ReLU as activation. We performed training batch-wise along with SGD optimizer where size of each batch is 32 on a single GPU. Though Adam [18] could be an alternative of SGD for faster convergence. Weights initialization of our all models happened randomly as we trained our network from scratch. We followed the strategy explained in [19]. Regarding other network configuration, weight decay and momentum were set to 0.0001 and 0.9 respectively and we maintained the same hyper-parameters across all models. We started training with initial learning rate as 0.1 and employed standard polynomial decay strategy to decrease this value over 350K iterations. To implement group convolution, we used parameter "group" that is supported in Caffe. We did not use dropout [20] in our models. For all experiments, we used NVIDIA Titan X 12G GPU with 24 GB RAM.

In testing phase, we resize the image to 224×224 and didn't take horizontal flip. However, per channel mean subtraction is done as per standard mean for R, G, and B channels available for ImageNet database [8].

4   Experimental Study

We performed our set of experiments on ImageNet classification dataset [8] that consists of 1000 classes. As our intention is to evaluate the efficacy of aggregated or group convolution for lightweight deep networks, we proceed with a brief overview of the technique its background. As mentioned in [12], the idea of group convolution was first used in AlexNet architecture [8]. However, the purpose was not to enhance the performance, rather Krizhevsky et al. tried to implement the network over two GPUs. So that two sets of convolution operations can be performed in parallel and later the convolved feature maps can be merged using fully connected layers. This approach was followed back in 2012 as the GPU had limited capacity. However, Xie et al. [12] made the first attempt to use this concept to boost up the accuracy with much deeper network. They referred to the number of groups as cardinality and it is considered as a new dimension to the deep neural network. Later in 2017, this idea was perceived as shuffling the channels after performing group convolution to blend the features across groups [15].

In neural networks, a single neuron receives input from multiple channels and a simple transformation namely inner product of neuron inputs and its weights is performed:

$$\sum_{i=1}^{N} x_i * w_i \tag{1}$$

where x is a set of input channels to a single neuron. Hence $x = [x_1, x_2, x_3, ..., x_N]$ and likewise a set of filters' weights will be there of same dimension. Here, subscript denotes the channel. This simple transformation can be replaced by a more generic function where each element can be considered as a mini-network. The transformation is designed in such a way that the network expands along a new dimension, it was defined as cardinality and the concept is known as "Network-in-*Neuron*". Instead of number of channels, if Eq. (1) can be expanded in number of groups where each group will have a certain number of channels then we can conceptualize about a new aggregated transformation as explained in [12]. Figure 2 shows two different networks. The network at the left is a basic residual like block where X is the input and output depth that is number of channels. In between the input and the output, there are three convolution layers where convolution with a kernel size of 1×1 is used to increase or decrease the number of channels. It is also used to blend the features across channels and convolution with a kernel size of 3×3. However, kernel size for feature extraction can be changed as needed. The function defined below shows the factor by which the increment of channel is performed.

$$f : X \rightarrow X^*, X \in \mathbb{R}^{H*W*D}, X^* \in \mathbb{R}^{H'*W'*D'} \tag{2}$$

$$f' : X^* \rightarrow X^*, X^* \in \mathbb{R}^{H'*W'*D'}, X^* \in \mathbb{R}^{H''*W''*D''} \tag{3}$$

where X and X^* are input and output of transformation function f. H, W, D are the height, width and depth of X and H', W', D' are the height, width and depth of X^*. Transformation function f' is used to extract features keeping depth or number of channels constant. To decrease the number of channels, generally $D' = D/r$ where r is an integer value which is ideally a factor of 4 . Same rule in reverse order has to be followed while increasing the number of channels as it will be required in the third convolution layer as shown in Fig. 1. It is to be noted that f, f' and reverse of f will be the same across groups. It is demonstrated as in [12], with increasing number of groups the accuracy is more likely to improve with reduced model size.

4.1 Aggregated vs. 3D Convolution

As discussed in previous section, aggregated residual transformation has seen to be superior in terms of performance than normal 3D convolution. While this study is purely concentrated on deep networks, it was interesting to study it in a non-deep network. The experimental results revealed some compelling facts to think on having such features on a lightweight embedded friendly network. It is

Table 1. Comparison study: aggregated vs. 3D convolution

Type of layer/block	Output	ResNeXt-12	ResNeXt-12 without group convolution
Conv.	112 × 112	(5 × 5, 32)/2	(5 × 5, 32)/2
Pool.	56 × 56	(2 × 2 max pool)/2	(2 × 2 max pool)/2
BSC	56 × 56	(3 × 3, 32, C = 4), (1 × 1, 32)	(3 × 3, 32), (1 × 1, 32)
BIC	28 × 28	(3 × 3, 64, C = 16)/2, (1 × 1, 64), IC: (1 × 1, 64)/2	(3 × 3, 64)/2, (1 × 1, 64), IC: (1 × 1, 64)/2
BIC	14 × 14	(3 × 3, 128, C = 32)/2, (1 × 1, 128), IC: (1 × 1, 128)/2	(3 × 3, 128)/2, (1 × 1, 128)/2, IC: (1 × 1, 128)/2
BIC	7 × 7	(3 × 3, 256, C = 64)/2, (1 × 1, 256), IC: (1 × 1, 256)/2	(3 × 3, 256)/2, (1 × 1, 256), IC: (1 × 1, 256)/2
	1 × 1	Global average pool1000-d fc, softmax	Global average pool1000-d fc, softmax
#params.		402.73k	788.65k
TOP-1 accuracy		37.72	48.59

Table 2. Comparison study: group convolution with skip vs. non-skip connections

Type of layer/block	Group convolution with skip connection	Group convolution without skip connection
Conv.	(5 × 5, 64)/2, (O = 112 × 112)	(5 × 5, 64)/2, (O = 112 × 112)
Pool.	(2 × 2 max pool)/2, (O = 56 × 56)	(2 × 2 max pool)/2, (O = 56 × 56)
BSC	(5 × 5, 64), (5 × 5, 64, C = 4), (O = 56 × 56)	(5 × 5, 64), (5 × 5, 64, C = 4), (O = 56 × 56)
BIC	(5 × 5, 64)/2, (5 × 5, 64, C = 4), IC: (1 × 1, 64)/2, (O = 28 × 28)	(5 × 5, 128)/2, (O = 28 × 28) (5 × 5, 128, C = 4) (O = 28 × 28)
BIC	(5 × 5, 128)/2, (5 × 5, 128, C = 4), IC: (1 × 1, 128)/2, (O = 14 × 14)	(5 × 5, 128)/2, (O = 14 × 14) (5 × 5, 128, C = 4) (O=14 × 14)
BIC	(5 × 5, 256)/2, (5 × 5, 256, C = 4), IC: (1 × 1, 256)/2, (O = 7 × 7)	(5 × 5, 256)/2, (O = 7 × 7), (5 × 5, 256, C = 4), (O = 7 × 7)
	Global average pool1000-d fc, softmax, O = 1 × 1	Global average pool1000-d fc, softmax, O = 1 × 1
#params.	2.1M	2.44M
TOP-1 accuracy	57.4619	58.606

Table 3. Comparison study: group convolution with deeper vs. wider network of similar depth

Type of layer/block	Output	Group convolution with deeper network	Group convolution with wider network of similar depth
Conv.	112×112	$(5 \times 5, 32)/2$	$(5 \times 5, 32)/2$
Pool.	56×56	$(2 \times 2$ max pool$)/2$	$(2 \times 2$ max pool$)/2$
BSC	56×56	$(5 \times 5, 32)(5 \times 5, 32, C = 4)$	$(5 \times 5, 32)(5 \times 5, 32, C = 4)$
BIC	28×28	$(5 \times 5, 32)/2, (5 \times 5, C = 4)(1 \times 1, 64)$ IC: $(1 \times 1, 64)/2$	$(5 \times 5, 32)/2, (5 \times 5, 32, C = 4)(1 \times 1, 64)$ IC: $(1 \times 1, 64)/2$
BIC	14×14	$(5 \times 5, 64)/2, (5 \times 5, 64, C = 8)(1 \times 1, 256)$ IC: $(1 \times 1, 128)/2$	$(5 \times 5, 128)/2, (5 \times 5, 128, C = 8)(1 \times 1, 256)$ IC: $(1 \times 1, 256)/2$
BIC	7×7	$(5 \times 5, 128)/2, (5 \times 5, 128, C = 16)(1 \times 1, 256)$ IC: $(1 \times 1, 256)/2$	$(5 \times 5, 256)/2, (5 \times 5, 256, C = 16)(1 \times 1, 512)$ IC: $(1 \times 1, 512)/2$
	1×1	Global average pool1000-d fc, softmax	Global average pool1000-d fc, softmax
#params.		1.75M	6.04M
TOP-1 accuracy		52.718	59.4601

Table 4. Comparison study: incremental vs. wider network of similar depth

Type of layer/block	Output	Deeper network with incremental growth	Deeper network with double growth
Conv.	112×112	$(5 \times 5, 32)/2$	$(5 \times 5, 64)/2$
Pool.	56×56	$(2 \times 2$ max pool$)/2$	$(2 \times 2$ max pool$)/2$
Conv.	56×56	$(5 \times 5, 32)(5 \times 5, 32)$	$(5 \times 5, 64)(5 \times 5, 64)$
Conv.	28×28	$(5 \times 5, 64)/2, (5 \times 5, 64)$	$(5 \times 5, 128)/2, (5 \times 5, 128)$
Conv.	14×14	$(5 \times 5, 128)/2, (5 \times 5, 128)$	$(5 \times 5, 256)/2, (5 \times 5, 256)$
Conv.	7×7	$(5 \times 5, 256)/2, (5 \times 5, 256)$	$(5 \times 5, 512)/2, (5 \times 5, 512)$
	1×1	Global average pool1000-d fc, softmax	Global average pool1000-d fc, softmax
#params.		3.51M	13.53M
TOP-1 accuracy		57.42	65.5301

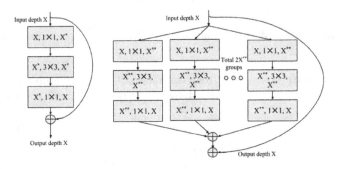

Fig. 2. Residual block with (1) 3D convolution (left) and (2) aggregated convolution (right)

to be noted that we performed group convolution at all layers except the 1×1 convolution layers.

We adopted two modularized 12 layers residual networks. Just to see the efficacy of group convolution, we added this feature in only one network. In the model, we have two types of residual networks. One type of residual block contains two consecutive convolution layers and other type has only skip connections. Later both meet at the same point to sum up the features and have non-linearity through ReLU. We refer to this block as 'Block of Static Channel' (BSC). In another kind of residual block, two consecutive convolution layers are used where network width will be increased. In order to match such increment in channel, another convolution (denoted as IC in Table 1) will be added in the parallel skip connection. In the same way, both connections will meet at the same point to sum up the features and have non-linearity through ReLU. We call this block 'Block of Incremental Channel' (BIC). Figure 3 clearly shows the difference between BSC (left) and BIC (right) type of network.

In Table 1, "(" and ")" denote the start and end of a layer. Within each set of these brackets kernel size, number of output channels, number of groups, type of pooling are mentioned. Stride is represented as "/2". ResNeXt-12 refers to a residual network that includes one BSC and repetitive BIC blocks. Group convolution (denoted by "C" in Table 1) is used mainly in BIC blocks. The other network at the right side shares similar network architecture but it does not use group convolution. From Table 1, it is clear that even though aggregated transformation reduces hyper-parameters in large scale but definitely it is not a suitable candidate to have in lightweight network.

4.2   Group Convolution with Skip vs. Non-skip Connection

Skip connection has been in heavy use since it was introduced in ResNet [11]. Various studies on the impact of skip connection in larger network are well documented. However, we could not find any literature that experimented on this type of connection in lightweight deep network. It became a matter of our utmost interest to see how group convolution is effective for smaller networks

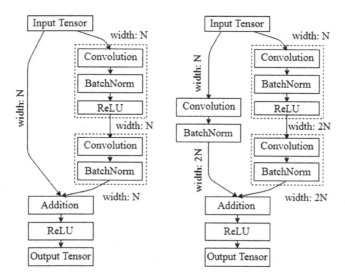

Fig. 3. Two types of residual block (1) block of static channel (left) and (2) block of incremental channel (right)

with and without skip connections. We considered this experiment to be very important as skip connections on embedded platform make the network heavy as it requires more memory and it makes the network considerably slow. When we introduce skip connections in the network, the feature maps to be retrieved later for feature summation will be saved in a storage space. When the feature maps need to be retrieved, then DMA (Direct Memory Access) will try to copy the data in the cache memory which is generally very small. If the size of the data is larger and can not be accommodated in cache then DMA will keep on copying data partially to cache memory and process the same. Hence, more channels will make the DMA to perform the above mentioned rolling buffer operation quite a number of times. So this approach will ultimately result in having higher inference time and we are not left with any workaround for such a problem. Table 2 demonstrates the network configuration of two networks that use group convolution but one uses skip and other non-skip connections.

We presented two near similar networks, one with skip connections and other without skip connections. We maintained the same notations that we used in Table 1. We introduced a new notation "O" that refers to the output dimension. For the network without skip connections, the output dimension is mentioned after each layer in the table. The results from both networks are indeed intriguing.

4.3 Group Convolution with Incremental vs. Drastic Growth in Width

Constructing a deeper network while preventing overfitting is a topic of discussion in the research community. Techniques to deepen a network has been studied extensively [11,12,21,22]. In order to go deeper, we need to make sure we have adequate data, reasonable feature space and that the network converges without overfitting. The set of experiments that we have presented till now, have feature space of size 7 × 7 at the last convolution layer. With even small filters it is meaningless to make the architecture go deeper. So instead of going deeper we plan to go wider with a drastic change in width. So we experimented with two networks of similar depth but with different width. Topology details of these two networks are furnished in Table 3.

We demonstrated the efficacy of dramatic increment of number of channels with group convolution. We maintained the same notations as in Tables 1 and 2. The result of this experiment certainly helps to understand about the impact of a less experimented dimension that is width in lightweight deep network. It is now clear that if we can not go deeper then to boost the performance, going wider is an option. Though it is unarguably true that the network will become more expensive, it is balanced by the impressive gain in accuracy.

4.4 3D Convolution with Incremental vs. Double Growth in Width

In continuation with the last experiment, it was fascinating to have an insight on the drastic growth in width of a relatively smaller network. The result reveals that there is good benefit on having such growth in the network while imbibing group convolution and skip connections. So it became our further interest to see instead of having dramatic growth in width how the network performs if the width is just doubled from the original network without using group convolution and skip connection. To have an understanding about the impact after such a change in the network, we experimented with two different convolution neural networks of similar depth. In one network, the growth in width is gradual but in the other one the width is just double per layer than in the first network. Network details along with results are provided in Table 4. The results clearly indicate that making a smaller network wider has an advantage over relatively a thin network.

5   Conclusion

In this work, we provided a detailed study of group convolution technique for smaller networks suitable for embedded systems. We constructed several networks to systematically study the effect of width, depth, skip connection for group convolution networks. We share our study to show that design techniques suitable for deeper networks may not apply to shallower networks. Our experiments on the lightweight networks can be summarized as follows: (1) group convolution was found to significantly worse than the regular 3D convolution, (2) skip connections provided only a small improvement in accuracy in shallower networks and (3) increasing the width of the network produces significant improvement in accuracy. In future work, we plan to encode all the various parameterizations into a meta-architecture where the optimal configuration can be explored via meta-learning instead of manual configuration and experimentation.

References

1. Briot, A., AI, G., Creteil, V., Viswanath, P., Yogamani, S.: Analysis of efficient cnn design techniques for semantic segmentation. In: Proceedings of the IEEE Conference on Computer Vision and Pattern Recognition Workshops, pp. 663–672 (2018)
2. Iandola, F.N., Keutzer, K.: Keynote: small neural nets are beautiful: enabling embedded systems with small deep-neural-network architectures. CoRR abs/1710.02759 (2017)
3. Canziani, A., Paszke, A., Culurciello, E.: An analysis of deep neural network models for practical applications. CoRR abs/1605.07678 (2016)
4. Huang, J., et al.: Speed/accuracy trade-offs for modern convolutional object detectors. CoRR abs/1611.10012 (2016)
5. LeCun, Y., et al.: Backpropagation applied to handwritten zip code recognition. Neural Comput. **1**(4), 541–551 (1989)
6. Lowe, D.G.: Distinctive image features from scale-invariant keypoints. Int. J. Comput. Vis. **60**(2), 91–110 (2004)
7. Dalal, N., Triggs, B.: Histograms of oriented gradients for human detection. In: Proceedings of the 2005 IEEE Computer Society Conference on Computer Vision and Pattern Recognition, CVPR 2005 (2005)
8. Krizhevsky, A., Sutskever, I., Hinton, G.E.: ImageNet classification with deep convolutional neural networks. In: 25th International Conference on Neural Information Processing Systems, USA (2012)
9. Lin, M., Chen, Q., Yan, S.: Network in network. CoRR (2013)
10. Simonyan, K., Zisserman, A.: Very deep convolutional networks for large-scale image recognition. CoRR (2014)
11. He, K., Zhang, X., Ren, S., Sun, J.: Deep residual learning for image recognition. In: 2016 IEEE Conference on Computer Vision and Pattern Recognition (CVPR), pp. 770–778 (2016)
12. Xie, S., Girshick, R.B., Dollár, P., Tu, Z., He, K.: Aggregated residual transformations for deep neural networks. CoRR abs/1611.05431 (2016)
13. Szegedy, C., Ioffe, S., Vanhoucke, V.: Inception-v4, inception-ResNet and the impact of residual connections on learning. CoRR (2016)
14. Iandola, F.N., Moskewicz, M.W., Ashraf, K., Han, S., Dally, W.J., Keutzer, K.: SqueezeNet: AlexNet-level accuracy with 50x fewer parameters and <1mb model size. CoRR (2016)
15. Zhang, X., Zhou, X., Lin, M., Sun, J.: ShuffleNet: an extremely efficient convolutional neural network for mobile devices. CoRR (2017)
16. Jia, Y., et al.: Caffe: convolutional architecture for fast feature embedding. In: Proceedings of the 22nd ACM International Conference on Multimedia, MM 2014, pp. 675–678 (2014)

17. Ioffe, S., Szegedy, C.: Batch normalization: accelerating deep network training by reducing internal covariate shift, pp. 448–456 (2015)
18. Kingma, D.P., Ba, J.: Adam: a method for stochastic optimization. CoRR abs/1412.6980 (2014)
19. He, K., Zhang, X., Ren, S., Sun, J.: Delving deep into rectifiers: surpassing human-level performance on ImageNet classification. In: Proceedings of the 2015 IEEE International Conference on Computer Vision (ICCV) (2015)
20. Srivastava, N., Hinton, G., Krizhevsky, A., Sutskever, I., Salakhutdinov, R.: Dropout: a simple way to prevent neural networks from overfitting. J. Mach. Learn. Res.
21. Roy, S., Das, N., Kundu, M., Nasipuri, M.: Handwritten isolated Bangla compound character recognition: a new benchmark using a novel deep learning approach. Pattern Recognition Lett. **90**, 15–21 (2017)
22. Roy, S., Das, A., Bhattacharya, U.: Generalized stacking of layerwise-trained deep convolutional neural networks for document image classification. In: 23rd International Conference on Pattern Recognition, ICPR 2016 (2016)

Image-Based Driver Drowsiness Detection

F. Dornaika[1,2(✉)], F. Khattar[1], J. Reta[1], I. Arganda-Carreras[1,2],
M. Hernandez[1], and Y. Ruichek[3]

[1] University of the Basque Country UPV/EHU, San Sebastian, Spain
`fadi.dornaika@ehu.es`
[2] IKERBASQUE, Basque Foundation for Science, Bilbao, Spain
[3] LE2i, CNRS, University of Bourgogne Franche-Comte, Belfort, France

Abstract. How to extract effective features of fatigue in images and videos is important for many applications. This paper introduces a face image descriptor that can be used for discriminating driver fatigue in static frames. In this method, first, each facial image in the sequence is represented by a pyramid whose levels are divided into non-overlapping blocks of the same size, and hybrid image descriptor are employed to extract features in all blocks. Then the obtained descriptor is filtered out using feature selection. Finally, non-linear Support Vector Machines is applied to predict the drowsiness state of the subject in the image. The proposed method was tested on the public dataset NTH Drowsy Driver Detection (NTHUDDD). This dataset includes a wide range of human subjects of different genders, poses, and illuminations in real-life fatigue conditions. Experimental results show the effectiveness of the proposed method. These results show that the proposed hand-crafted feature compare favorably with several approaches based on the use of deep Convolutional Neural Nets.

Keywords: Drowsiness detection · Hand-crafted features ·
Deep features · Supervised classification

1 Introduction

Three categories of methods can be deployed in order to detect driver fatigue [1–3]. The first category groups all methods that are based on some physiological information like electrocardiogram (ECG), electroencephalogram (EEG), and blood pressure [4]. The second category groups methods that identify the driver status from interaction with the vehicle, including driver's grip force on the steering wheel, speed, acceleration, and braking. The third category relies on the use of computer vision techniques in order te identify the driver's status via the deployment of cameras and optical sensors [5–8]. The first category can give high recognition accuracy but is not easy to be adopted by drivers as it is intrusive to measure the breathing and heart rates and the brain activity. The second category can be non-intrusive but it is subject to many limitations, including vehicle type, driver experience and external conditions. On the other

© Springer Nature Switzerland AG 2019
X. Bai et al. (Eds.): FFER 2018/DLPR 2018, LNCS 11264, pp. 61–71, 2019.
https://doi.org/10.1007/978-3-030-12177-8_6

hand, the computer vision technology is non-invasive and is merely based on the driver behavior. This technology becomes more and more practical.

In recent drowsy driver detection systems, the main work focuses on using limited visual cues (often just one). However, human drowsiness is a complicated mechanism. Many existing works for vision-based driver fatigue detection focus only on attributes of eyes or mouth [5,9–11]. It is assumed that drowsiness state corresponds to rapid and constant blinking, nodding or head swinging, and frequent yawning. Thus, the extracted features could not well encode the state of driver drowsiness. These approaches are entirely depending on a good and accurate location of the eyes and mouth, which can be very challenging in the real-life driving condition. The simplest method to predict drowsiness level is to set a threshold on extracted drowsiness-related symptoms. In the system presented in [12], the percentage of eyelid closure (PERCLOS) in a time window has shown to provide meaningful message of drowsiness. Teyeb et al. [13] showed that when the head inclination angle exceeds a certain value and duration, the level of alertness of the driver is lowered. In [10], yawning is detected based on the rate of change of the mouth contour and is determined as the only sign of drowsiness. This approach may encounter false-alarms when the required visual cues cannot be distinguished from the similar motions, e.g. talking or laughing. In [14], the authors developed a gaze zone detection algorithm based on features learnt using a convolutional neural network. Based on these features, support vector machine (SVM) is used to estimate driver gaze zone. In addition to the mentioned works, some researchers consider the texture dynamics [15–19].

In this paper, we propose a hand-crafted face descriptor that exploits different scales and different image regions of the face. For each level and for each image region, a compact and hybrid texture descriptor is applied. This is given by the covariance description over a set of raw features (image derivatives, Local Binary Patterns, etc.). The face descriptor is given by the concatenation of all regions. Figure 1 illustrates the flowchart of our proposed scheme.

The paper is organized as follows. Section 2 presents the adopted 2D face alignment. Section 3 describes the proposed descriptor. Section 4 illustrates experimental results obtained with the public dataset NTH Drowsy Driver Detection. Section 5 concludes the paper.

2   Face Alignment

Face alignment is one of the most important stages in face image analysis. In our work, the eyes of each face are detected using the Ensemble of Regression Trees (ERT) algorithm [20] which is a robust and very efficient algorithm for facial landmarks localization.

Once we have the 2D positions of the two eyes, we use them to compensate for the in-plane rotation of the face. To this end, within the detected face region, the positions of right and left eyes are located as (R_x, R_y) and (L_x, L_y), respectively. Then, the angle of in-plane rotation is calculated by $\theta = artan(\frac{R_y - L_y}{R_x - L_x})$, and the input face region is rotated by the that angle.

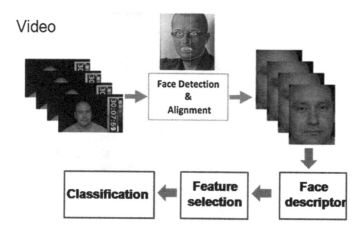

Fig. 1. A schematic representation of data flow for drowsiness detection in individual video frames.

After rotation correction, we use a global scale for the face image, this scale normalizes the inter-ocular distance to a fixed value l. The latter sets the scale of the face in the obtained image. After performing the rotation and rescaling, the face region should be cropped (aligned face). To this end, a bounding box is centered on the new eyes location (on the transformed face image) and then stretched to the left and to the right by $k_0 \cdot l$, and to top by $k_1 \cdot l$ and to bottom by $k_2 \cdot l$. Finally, in our case, k_0, k_1, k_2 and l are chosen such that the final face image has a size of 250×250 pixels. Figure 2 illustrates the 2D alignment of a given face.

3 Proposed Face Feature

3.1 Covariance Descriptor

The original covariance descriptor is a statistic based feature proposed by [21] for generic object detection and texture classification tasks. Instead of using histograms, they compute the covariance matrices among the color channels and gradient images. Compared with other descriptors, the covariance descriptor lies in a very low-dimensional space, and gives a natural way of fusing multiples types of features as long as they can be presented spatially. Thus, this descriptor can benefit from any progress made in image feature extraction. In addition, this descriptor lends itself nicely to efficient implementation whenever the image regions are rectangular by exploiting the integral image concept as it is described in [21].

Since its introduction the covariance descriptor has not received much attention by researchers despite its ability to incorporate a large number of existing and recent texture features. This motivates us to propose an extension of

(a) Original frame.

(b) Aligned and cropped face.

Fig. 2. Face alignment and cropping associated with one original face image in the public dataset NTH Drowsy Driver Detection (NTHUDDD).

this descriptor that includes two new aspects. First, we compute the covariance matrices using texture descriptors such as Local Binary Pattern and Local Phase Quantization images. Second, we exploit this covariance descriptor using a Pyramid-Multi Level (PML) face representation which allows a multi-level multi scale feature extraction. The PML representation will be described in the next section.

3.2 Proposed Pyramid Multi-level Descriptor

The PML Descriptor (PMLD) adopts an explicit pyramid representation generated from the original aligned face image. This pyramid characterizes the image at different scales. At each level, the image is divided in an appropriate number of square blocks (sub-images). The descriptor of each block is then extracted. The PMLD relies on the concatenation of the multi-block representation performed at each level.

In the sequel, we define the ℓ-PML Descriptor. For simplification of the model formalization, we consider the case of square images. The methods can easily be generalized to rectangular images (Fig. 3).

Let f be an image of size $N \times N$. Let P be its pyramid representation with ℓ levels, $P = \{P_1, \cdots, P_\ell\}$ [22]. The size of the images P_i should meet the following. Each level P_i is represented by a partition of square blocks of size

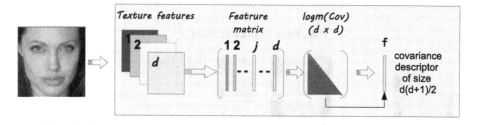

Fig. 3. A schematic representation of the covariance descriptor. The input face image is represented by a set of d texture and color features that will be fused in the final covariance descriptor.

$\frac{N}{\ell} \times \frac{N}{\ell}$, $P_i = \{B_{i,1}, \cdots, B_{i,n_i}\}$, where $n_i = i^2$. Given a value ℓ, we pose $b = \frac{N}{\ell}$. Thus, the size of square blocks at all levels is $b \times b$. We point out that P_ℓ is f and $P_1 = B_{1,1}$ (coarsest resolution).

The pyramid representation of an image f by ℓ levels is the sequence $L_1, \ldots, L_\ell$ such that:

$$L_i = \{B_{i,1}, \ldots, B_{i,n_i}\} \text{ where } i = 1, \ldots, \ell$$

At each level, the local features of each block are described by the covariance descriptor presented in the previous section. Concretely, the PML Descriptor at the level i ($i = 1, \ldots, \ell$) is given by:

$$\mathrm{COV}(L_i) = \mathrm{COV}(B_{i,1}) \| \cdots \| \mathrm{COV}(B_{i,n_i})$$

where $\|$ denotes the concatenation operator. Therefore, we define the PML Descriptor using ℓ levels of the pyramid representation as follows:

$$\ell\text{-PMLD}(f) = \mathrm{COV}(L_1) \| \ldots \| \mathrm{COV}(L_\ell)$$

We can observe that the total number of blocks in a pyramid of depth ℓ is $\sum_{i=1}^{\ell} i^2 = \frac{\ell(\ell+1)(2\ell+1)}{6}$. Hence, ℓ-PMLD is composed of $\frac{d(d+1)}{2} \frac{\ell(\ell+1)(2\ell+1)}{6}$ elements, since the number of elements of COV descriptor is $\frac{d(d+1)}{2}$.

Figure 4 illustrates the principle of the 3-PMLD associated with an aligned face image.

3.3 Feature Selection

The obtained face descriptor may contain some spurious or redundant features that can hinder the discrimination of the final classifier. Thus, before learning a classifier a feature selection approach is invoked in order to select the most relevant features. We use Fisher scoring of the features in order to extract the most relevant and discriminative features of the PML-based descriptors. Fisher

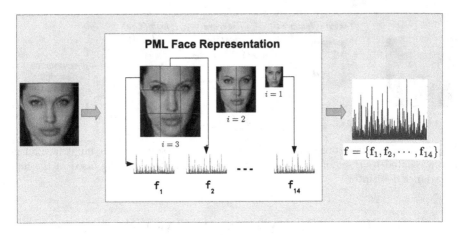

Fig. 4. Pyramid Multi-Level (PML) covariance descriptor for a pyramid of three levels. At each level i the image is divided into i^2 blocks resulting to a total number of blocks given by $B = \sum_{i=1}^{\ell} i^2 = \ell(\ell+1)(2\ell+1)/6$. For each block a regional multi-block covariance descriptor ($\mathbf{f_i}$) is extracted and finally the PML-based feature descriptor is obtained by concatenating all regional descriptors ($\mathbf{f} = \{\mathbf{f_1}, \mathbf{f_2}, \ldots, \mathbf{f_B}\}$).

method is a supervised feature selection method which uses class labels to identify features with best discriminant ability. Let $\mathbf{z} \in \mathbb{R}^D$ denote the PML descriptor associated with a face image. The Fisher score of the rth feature is given by:

$$F_r = \frac{N_1\left(\mu_{r,1} - \mu_r\right)^2 + N_2\left(\mu_{r,2} - \mu_r\right)^2}{N_1\,\sigma_{r,1}^2 + N_2\,\sigma_{r,2}^2} \quad r = 1, \ldots, D \tag{1}$$

where N_1 and N_2 are respectively the number of positive and negative images. $\mu_{r,1}$ and $\sigma_{r,1}^2$ refer to the mean and variance of the rth feature of the positive class, and $\mu_{r,2}$ and $\sigma_{r,2}^2$ refer to the mean and variance of the rth feature of the negative class. μ_r refers to the global mean of the rth feature. Here the positive class refers to the drowsy state while the negative class refers to the non drowsy state.

The output of the feature selection is a vector of real scores that can gives a ranking of the attributes composing the PML covariance descriptor. From this obtained ordering, several feature subsets can be chosen by setting a cutoff for the selected features. In our work, we have adopted threshold-based criterion. In fact, we have analyzed different cutoff values ranging from 10 to 90% of the relevant features. Once the selection is fixed, it is applied on both the training and test sets. In our work, the pyramid level is set to five, and the number of low level image features is 19.

4   Experimental Setup

4.1   Dataset

Despite the importance of research in a practical drowsy driver detection system, most research have used relatively limited datasets. The generalization of different approaches to drowsy driver detection analysis remains unknown. In the absence of performance evaluation on a common public dataset, the comparative strength and weakness of different approaches is difficult to determine. Furthermore, most of the proposed approaches have drawbacks due to impractical reasons or do not provide sufficient discrimination to capture the uncertainties. Moreover, most of the existing methods do not evaluate the robustness of their system against subjects from different ethnicities, races, genders, various illumination conditions and partial occlusion (e.g. glasses, sun-glasses and facial hair).

In our study, the public dataset NTH Drowsy Driver Detection (NTHUDDD) [23] is used. This video dataset contains 36 subjects including different people, both genders, different ethnicities, which is in five situations as shown in Fig. 5. Each situation contains at least two behaviors about drowsy states, such as slow blinking, nodding, and yawning as shown in Fig. 6.

Fig. 5. Example frames of different situations (night wearing glasses, night bareface, wearing glasses, wearing sunglasses, bareface) and same behavior (drowsy state) from 5 video clips [23].

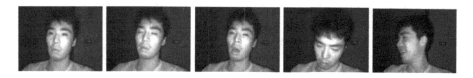

Fig. 6. Example frames of same situation (night bareface) and different behaviors (mixing drowsy and non-drowsy state) from one video clip [23].

The total dataset consists of train dataset, evaluation dataset, and test dataset. The train dataset consists of 360 video clips (722, 223 frames) of 18 subjects. The evaluation dataset consists of 20 video clips (173, 259 frames) of 4 subjects and test dataset consists of 70 clips (736, 132 frames) of 14 subjects. During training and evaluation, each frame is binary labeled: drowsy or nondrowsy.

The ground-truth label for test dataset is not publicly available yet. The dataset includes different physical attributes including variety in skin tone, fatigue, facial structure, clothes and hair styles. The videos are in 640 × 480 pixels, 30 frames per second AVI format without audio.

5   Experimental Results

We compare the proposed approach with the following deep neural nets [23]:

- 8-layered AlexNet: This net consists of 5 convolution layers and 3 fully connected layers which has 60 million parameters and 650,000 neurons, and this model is trained with 1.2 million images for 1000 categories classification This net is fine tuned using the training images of (NTHUDDD) dataset.
- VGG-Face: The VGG-FaceNet is trained to learn facial feature related to drowsiness which is robust to genders, ethnicity, hair style and various accessories adornment.
- FlowImageNet: This net takes dense optical flow image that is extracted from consecutive image sequences and is trained to learn behavior features related to drowsiness such as facial and head movements.

These three networks are independently fine-tunned for multi-class drowsiness classification given the following four classes: non-drowsiness, drowsiness with eye blinking, nodding, and yawning. Two different fusion strategies were considered: independently-averaged architecture (IAA) and feature-fused architecture (FFA). During IAA, the probability distributions of each network output for multi-class classification are integrated, and average probabilities are used to determine the driver drowsiness. During FFA, the three networks are also integrated such that their FC7 layer features are concatenated, and based on this concatenated feature, input images are classified into one of four classes using SVM.

The proposed method aims to classify each frame in videos based on feature representation learning. Due to the lack of ground truth label of test dataset, we substituted evaluation dataset for test data. The adopted protocol is similar to the one depicted in [23]. In particular, in order to simplify the training process, the training video sequences are sub-sampled by a factor of ten.

Table 1. Success rate (%) over the evaluation set of the Drowsy Driver Detection (NTHUDDD) 2016 dataset. The number of testing frames is 177,259.

Situation\ method	Alexnet	VGGFaceNet	FlowImageNet	LRCN [19]	DDD-FFA [23]	DDD-IA [23]	PML-COV
Bareface	70.42	63.87	56.33	68.75	79.41	69.83	**82.34**
Glasses	61.63	70.53	61.61	61.73	74.10	**75.93**	73.81
Sunglasses	70.20	57.00	67.57	71.47	61.89	69.86	**74.68**
Night-bareface	64.69	73.75	66.82	57.39	70.27	74.93	**79.35**
Night-glasses	62.70	74.10	55.17	55.63	68.37	**74.77**	69.29
Average	65.93	67.85	61.50	62.99	70.81	73.06	**75.90**

Table 1 summarizes the detection rate over the evaluation set using different approaches.

As it can be seen, the proposed approach outperformed all individual deep CNNs. In three situations the proposed methods outperformed the fusion scheme DDD-IA. In the two situations Glasses and Night-glasses the proposed scheme was outperformed by DDD-IA. The presence of glasses seem to be a perturbing factor in the proposed method.

Table 2. Confusion matrices obtained with the proposed descriptor. Each confusion matrix corresponds to a given situation.

Bareface		
Predicted	*Ground-truth*	
	Drowsy	**Non Drowsy**
Drowsy	18858	2111
Non Drowsy	5106	14780
Glasses		
Predicted	*Ground-truth*	
	Drowsy	**Non Drowsy**
Drowsy	14018	4779
Non Drowsy	4361	11741
Sunglasses		
Predicted	*Ground-truth*	
	Drowsy	**Non Drowsy**
Drowsy	9176	2528
Non Drowsy	4613	11893
Night-bareface		
Predicted	*Ground-truth*	
	Drowsy	**Non Drowsy**
Drowsy	14027	2709
Non Drowsy	2913	7582
Night-glasses		
Predicted	*Ground-truth*	
	Drowsy	**Non Drowsy**
Drowsy	10996	7993
Non Drowsy	2744	11185

Table 2 illustrates the obtained confusion matrices associated with the five situations. Except for the Sunglass situation, detecting the drowsiness seems to be more accurate than detecting the opposite state.

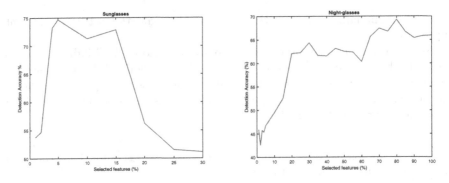

Fig. 7. Performance as a function of the selected features using Fisher scores.

Figure 7 illustrates the performance of our scheme as a function of the retained features after Fisher ranking. We can note that Principal Component Analysis (PCA) was applied on the raw COV descriptor before performing feature ranking.

6   Conclusion

Drowsiness detection is a key issue of a system for a vision-based driver fatigue monitoring. One of the main problems is how to extract and select effective features from face images. In this paper, multi-scale and multi-block features are used to extract fatigue features from the whole face, overcoming the defect of losing some important fatigue features when retrieving features from eyes or mouth only. Experimental results show that the proposed method can be equal or superior to several approaches that are based on deep Convolutional Neural Nets.

Experimental results show that the proposed face descriptor has a 75.90% detection accuracy on NTHU-drowsy driver detection benchmark dataset. Future work envisions the use of dynamic descriptors.

References

1. Azim, T., Jaffar, M.A., Mirza, A.M.: Fully automated real time fatigue detection of drivers through fuzzy expert systems. Appl. Soft Comput. **18**, 25–28 (2014)
2. Colic, A., Marques, O., Furht, B.: Driver Drowsiness Detection: Systems and Solutions. Springer, Heidelberg (2014). https://doi.org/10.1007/978-3-319-11535-1
3. Sigari, M., Pourshahabi, M., Soryani, M., Fathy, M.: A review on driver face monitoring systems for fatigue and distraction detection. Int. J. Adv. Sci. Technol. **64** (2014)
4. Awais, M., Badruddin, N., Drieberg, M.: A hybrid approach to detect driver drowsiness utilizing physiological signals to improve system performance and wearability. Sensors **17** (2017)

5. Sigari, M.H.: Driver hypo-vigilance detection based on eyelid behavior. In: International Conference on Advances in Pattern Recognition (2009)
6. Omidyeganeh, M., et al.: Yawning detection using embedded smart cameras. IEEE Trans. Instrum. Meas. **65**, 579–582 (2016)
7. Vesselenyi, T., Moca, S., Rus, A., Mitran, T., Tataru, B.: Driver drowsiness detection using ANN image processing. In: IOP Conference Series: Materials Science and Engineering, vol. 252 (2017)
8. Zhu, W., Yang, H., Jin, Y., Liu, B.: A method for recognizing fatigue driving based on Dempster-Shafer theory and fuzzy neural network. Math. Probl. Eng. (2017)
9. Kumar, N., Barwar, N.: Detection of eye blinking and yawning for monitoring driver's drowsiness in real time. Int. J. Appl. Innov. Eng. Manag. **3** (2014)
10. Alioua, N., Amine, A., Rziza, M.: Drivers fatigue detection based on yawning extraction. Int. J. Veh. Technol. (2014)
11. Bandara, I., Hudson, C.: Detection and tracking of eye blink to identify driver fatigue and napping. In: 20th British HCI Group Conference in Co-operation with ACM, HCI 2006: ENGAGE (2006)
12. Dasgupta, A., George, A., Happy, S., Routray, A.: A vision-based system for monitoring the loss of attention in automotive drivers. IEEE Trans. Intell. Transp. Syst. **14**, 1825–1838 (2013)
13. Teyeb, I., Jemai, O., Zaied, M., Ben Amar, C.: A drowsy driver detection system based on a new method of head posture estimation. In: Corchado, E., Lozano, J.A., Quintián, H., Yin, H. (eds.) IDEAL 2014. LNCS, vol. 8669, pp. 362–369. Springer, Cham (2014). https://doi.org/10.1007/978-3-319-10840-7_44
14. Choi, I.H., Hong, S.K., Kim, Y.G.: Real-time categorization of driver's gaze zone using the deep learning techniques. In: International Conference on Big Data and Smart Computing (BigComp) (2016)
15. Arashloo, S., Kittler, J.: Dynamic texture recognition using multiscale binarized statistical image features. IEEE Trans. Multimedia **16**, 2099–2109 (2014)
16. Päivärinta, J., Rahtu, E., Heikkilä, J.: Volume local phase quantization for blur-insensitive dynamic texture classification. In: Heyden, A., Kahl, F. (eds.) SCIA 2011. LNCS, vol. 6688, pp. 360–369. Springer, Heidelberg (2011). https://doi.org/10.1007/978-3-642-21227-7_34
17. Zhao, G., Pietikainen, M.: Dynamic texture recognition using local binary patterns with an application to facial expressions. IEEE Trans. Pattern Anal. Mach. Intell. **29**, 915–928 (2007)
18. Niu, G., Wang, C.: Driver fatigue features extraction. Math. Probl. Eng. (2014)
19. Donahue, J., et al.: Long-term recurrent convolutional networks for visual recognition and description. In: CVPR (2015)
20. Kazemi, V., Sullivan, J.: One millisecond face alignment with an ensemble of regression trees. In: IEEE Conference on Computer Vision and Pattern Recognition (2014)
21. Tuzel, O., Porikli, F., Meer, P.: A fast descriptor for detection and classification. In: European Conference on Computer Vision, pp. 589–600 (2006)
22. Szeliski, R.: Computer Vision Algorithms and Applications. Springer, London (2011). https://doi.org/10.1007/978-1-84882-935-0
23. Park, S., Pan, F., Kang, S., Yoo, C.D.: Driver drowsiness detection system based on feature representation learning using various deep networks. In: Asian Conference on Computer Vision Workshops (2016)

Continuous Presentation Attack Detection in Face Biometrics Based on Heart Rate

Javier Hernandez-Ortega(iD), Julian Fierrez(✉)(iD), Ester Gonzalez-Sosa(iD),
and Aythami Morales(iD)

Universidad Autonoma de Madrid, 28049 Madrid, Spain
{javier.hernandezo,julian.fierrez,aythami.morales}@uam.es
https://atvs.ii.uam.es/fierrez/

Abstract. In this paper we study face Presentation Attack Detection (PAD) against realistic 3D mask and high quality photo attacks in dynamic scenarios. We perform a comparison between a new pulse-based PAD approach based on a combination of a skin detector and a chrominance method, and the system used in our previous works (based on Blind Source Separation techniques, BSS). We also propose and study heuristical and statistical approaches for performing continuous PAD with low latency and false non-match rate. Results are reported using the 3D Mask Attack Database (3DMAD), and a self-collected dataset called BiDA Heart Rate Database (BiDA HR) including different video durations, resolutions, frame rates and attack artifacts. Several conclusions can be drawn from this work: (1) chrominance and BSS methods perform similarly under the controlled and favorable conditions found in 3DMAD and BiDA HR, (2) combining pulse information extracted from short-time sequences (e.g. 3 s) can be discriminant enough for performing the PAD task, (3) a high increase in PAD performance can be achieved with simple PAD score combination, and (4) the statistical method for continuous PAD outperforms the simple PAD score combination but it needs more data for building the statistical models.

Keywords: Face Presentation Attack Detection · Liveness detection · Continuous authentication

1 Introduction

Nowadays, face is one of the most extended biometric traits along with iris and fingerprint. The causes of this spread are the inherent properties of face-based systems: samples can be acquired at a distance, passively, continuously, and using legacy hardware. Faces also contain highly discriminant features in order to achieve high accuracy rates when performing the recognition and verification tasks. Other significant reason of this spread is the deployment of biometrics

© Springer Nature Switzerland AG 2019
X. Bai et al. (Eds.): FFER 2018/DLPR 2018, LNCS 11264, pp. 72–86, 2019.
https://doi.org/10.1007/978-3-030-12177-8_7

broadly for the first time. Face-based systems are now present in numerous scenarios like medical applications, video-surveillance, mobile devices, e-commerce, etc.

Because of those reasons, attacks to face recognition systems are now more than ever, an important security issue. Among all the types of attacks, presentation attacks consist in showing an artifact to the sensor (e.g. a camera) for trying to disguise the attacker as a genuine user of the biometric system [10].

Presentation Attack Detection (PAD) techniques deal with these type of attacks. Even though high detection results can be obtained with these methods, the same PAD techniques may not be useful against all types of artifacts [14]. One of the most harsh menaces existing today are Mask Attacks, in which the presentation attack artifact is a 3D mask of a genuine user's face [6]. In these attacks, most PAD techniques successful against photo and video attacks, e.g. texture and depth based, become useless for high quality masks, because their similar properties (geometry, color, shape) to their real counterparts.

More recently, remote PhotoPlethysmoGraphy (rPPG) techniques [17], consisting in analysing videos for extracting the user's pulse signal, have been employed to analyze video sequences, proving to be an effective countermeasure against 3D mask attacks [12]. However, in order to achieve a robust estimation of the pulse signal, published approaches that use this method need long video sequences, good light conditions, are sensitive to failures in the face detection module, and also dependent to different acquisition sensors.

Current approaches like [18] perform a short-time approach to rPPG, more adequate to variable scenarios, in which the user or attacking conditions can change in the middle of the video sequence. In particular, in continuous scenarios where the attacker can enter at any time in a video stream, short-time approaches to PAD permit low latency PAD decisions. In this case holistic approaches are unable to give a continuous estimation of pulse and/or presentation attack probability, or PAD decisions with low latency. In addition, a short-time analysis of the rPPG signal also allows a better subsequent processing of the rPPG signals toward an overall more robust long-term estimation of the pulse.

Classic authentication schemes, in which users are authenticated employing an initial login stage, are able to stop unauthorized access attempts, but they are still unable of avoiding session "hijacking". In these attacks, a genuine user has been correctly authenticated and accepted by the PAD module, but after that, an attacker may be able to get control of his session. This problem is specially relevant in the field of mobile authentication, where the portability of the devices makes easier their theft or loss.

Continuous Authentication has emerged in biometrics to deal with the mentioned security problems in mobile devices and personal computers. These techniques consist in monitoring the user in a continuous way for verifying that the current user is the same who made the initial login, ideally in a transparent manner. For accomplishing this objective, biometrics such as the face [16] or the touch interaction [7] can be captured continuously without the user being aware. Our proposed approach for PAD follows the same continuous strategy, but in

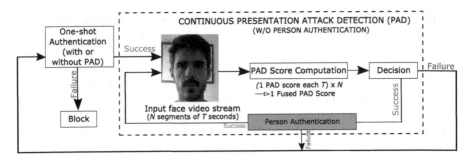

Fig. 1. Proposed scheme for Continuous Presentation Attack Detection (PAD). The authentication starts with a classic login (e.g. password, token or even a biometric trait), which may include or not PAD. If the login is successful, the continuous PAD loop starts working, generating PAD scores from the face video stream and deciding if a Presentation Attack has started or not. In the same loop we may also want to check also if the user is still the same (in gray), in a kind of Active Authentication scheme [16].

our case checking for PAD instead of identity. Please note that both identity and PAD can be incorporated in the loop, in a kind of continuous PAD and authentication scheme (see Fig. 1).

During a session hijacking, the attacker may be able to perform harmful actions, such as deleting or copying sensitive information, or installing a backdoor for granting future access to the compromised system. The latency of a continuous authentication method has the same level of criticalness than the accuracy rates, so a balance between usability and security must be achieved.

In this paper we: (1) present an algorithm based on rPPG for pulse detection applied to face Presentation Attack Detection (PAD); (2) study the performance of rPPG video-based continuous PAD, both in an existing benchmark (3DMAD) and a new dataset; and (3) test pulse-based continuous PAD in a scenario in which the attacking conditions vary over time.

The rest of this paper is organized as follows: Sect. 2 summarizes related works in rPPG and continuous authentication. Section 3 describes the proposed system. Section 4 describes the employed databases and the experimental protocol. Section 5 shows the results obtained. Finally, concluding remarks are drawn in Sect. 6.

2 Related Works

2.1 Remote Photoplethysmography

Photoplethysmography (PPG) [1] is a low-cost and noninvasive technique for measuring the cardiovascular Blood Volume Pulse (BVP) through variations in transmitted or reflected light. PPG can also be used to predict many vital health parameters such as blood pressure, heart rate (HR), hemoglobin and blood glucose level. Remote PPG (rPPG) consists in applying PPG techniques to video sequences. These techniques look for changes in the color of the user's face that are caused by changes in the concentration of oxygen in the blood.

Related to our work, Poh et al. [17] measured HR from videos captured with a web-cam. They tracked the user's face and performed ICA to the RGB signal to separate the BVP chrominance signal from the other illumination variations and noise. On the other hand, the CHROM method [5] performs a linear combination of the spectrum bands to map the PPG signals to a space in which they are more robust to artifacts and noise.

Other works like [19] localize and track the information of certain facial regions instead of the entire face as there exist some zones that present higher variations in their color due to the pulsations. In [15] they use a special sensor that has the capability to capture other two additional bands in the visible spectrum, since they have empirically proved to carry robustly the blood volume change information.

Regarding face PAD, when rPPG techniques are employed to estimate the pulse signal from a video sequence, the obtained result is highly different between the cases in which the recording contains a real face, and the cases with an attacking artifact (e.g. photos, videos, masks) [12].

Most research in this area employ self-collected datasets not publicly available. We decided to use 3DMAD as is one of the few public 3D mask PAD public datasets. It contains RGB videos of genuine users and of 3D mask attacks. We also employed a self-collected supplementary dataset in order to have larger RGB videos compared to the ones from 3DMAD. Larger recordings are necessary to measure the performance of continuous PAD techniques along time.

2.2   Continuous Authentication

A continuous authentication loop (see Fig. 1) can be added to any existing one-shot authentication system to improve its security. The most basic approach is based on using a single score in the authentication loop over time. The system generates a single score (i.e., $N = 1$ in Fig. 1) each T seconds and decides if there is another user (or a presentation attack) based on that single authentication (or PAD) score.

The next level of complexity consist in combining several scores (i.e., $N > 1$) using different types of logic. The first approximation is based on calculating the arithmetic mean of several consecutive scores and taking a decision based on that combination. The combination can be done in a more complex way, for example considering that the confidence in the presence of the user decays when the time since the last authentication increases, with a function that decreases with time. On the other hand, not all the video frames have the same quality, for example due to occlusions, movement, blur, etc. Confidence functions can be built taking into account the quality level of the extracted signals [2]. However, these heuristic methods are very specific to each scenario, and do not have high generalization capabilities.

One can also use statistical methods for integrating multiple authentication or PAD scores in the continuous loop of Fig. 1, by using gallery information to build models (typically real faces and attacks models for continuous PAD). Once the models are trained, the scores (single or multiple) that are extracted in the real environment are compared to the models in order to take a decision. A relevant work in this line is Quickest Change Detection (QCD). This technique has been employed successfully in mobile active authentication [7, 16] using multimodal data (i.e. face videos and touchscreen interaction).

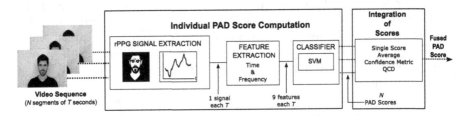

Fig. 2. Architecture of the proposed module for continuous pulse-based face presentation attack detection (PAD Score Computation in Fig. 1). Given a facial video (N segments of T seconds each, with a time overlap α), the face is detected and rPPG-related features are extracted from the ROI in order to obtain an individual PAD score of each considered video segment(of T seconds). Then, the considered video segment generates an individual PAD score considering a database of real faces and mask attacks using a SVM. Finally the individual PAD scores are combined to derive the final fused PAD score corresponding to the full input Video Sequence.

3   Proposed Approach

The main purpose of the continuous PAD module proposed in Fig. 1 consists in deciding if a video sequence contains images of real faces or images of presentation attacks. The architecture of this module is further detailed in Fig. 2. The first part is the rPPG signal extractor that obtains the pulse signal from the recordings. Once the rPPG signal is extracted from the video sequences, the second stage computes a set of features in order to distinguish between real faces and face attacks. The third step is a trained classifier that generates a score for each video sequence. The fourth and last stage integrates individual scores generated each T seconds, to form a final fused PAD Score each N individual scores.

3.1   rPPG Signal Extraction

The video sequences are generated from the input video stream by considering T seconds (with or without time overlap). The window length T allows to process larger or shorter pieces of the videos, having thus varying resolution in the final decision.

The rPPG signal generation is divided into two modules: skin detection and rPPG signal extraction:

Skin Detection. In the majority of the literature systems, the first stage consists in a face detection module (e.g. using the Viola-Jones algorithm) followed by ROI extraction. This stage selects one or several parts of the face that are assumed to contain robust information of the pulse signal. We applied this approach in our recent related work [11] and we have seen that it has several limitations such as: little robustness to movements, it can be difficult to implement, and it has a high computational load. Due to all these drawbacks, in this work we decided to apply the skin detector presented in [13] for getting our ROI. It transforms the video frames from the RGB color space to the YCrCb space. Their authors selected this color space as it has shown to have high discriminant properties for skin color modelling. The Y channel contains information of brightness while the Cr and Cb channels contain information about the differences between colors. A deeper description of the algorithm can be found in [13]. This algorithm skips a high number of pixels assuming that their values do not change within a small neighborhood. This approach reduce the CPU overload significantly making it suitable for real time video processing. Finally this algorithm does not depend of a face detection module, so it is more robust to user's movements.

rPPG Signal Extraction. Once the skin pixels have been located (see Fig. 3(c) and (d) for examples), the next stage consists in extracting the rPPG signal from each considered segment (of T seconds). First, the raw values of the pulse signal are computed as the average intensity of the skin pixels. This calculation is made for each frame of the segment and for each the three color channels: Red, Green and Blue. The outputs are three rPPG sequences, one for each color channel. These raw rPPG signals contain not only the light variations produced by the blood volume changes, but also variations due to the external illumination and other noise sources. To reduce those undesired factors, in [11] we processed each channel as follows: a detrending filter for reducing the slow non-pulsating changes in the rPPG signal, a moving-average filter for eliminating random noise, and a band-pass filter for magnifying the frequency bands related to the usual pulse values. In this present work we decided to use the CHROM algorithm [5], which performs a linear combination of the three individual color channels into only one signal, robust to noise and external interferences [5]. This method also performs a frequency analysis of the signal for magnifying the bands related to a expected human pulse (between 0.6 Hz and 4 Hz).

3.2 Feature Extraction

In our previous work [11], used for reference, we decided to use the features from [12], where the authors transformed the signal from the spatial domain to the frequency domain using the FFT, and after that they estimated its Power Spectral Density (PSD) distribution. Two features were extracted from each color band: the maximum power response P, and the ratio R between P and the total power in the 0.6–4 Hz frequency range.

For this work we decided to complement these two features P and R with other discriminant features that can give us more information about the rPPG signal in the time domain, following [4]. That work processed data from 3D accelerometer sensors, but their analysis is extrapolable to our rPPG signals. The final selected features can be seen in Table 1.

Table 1. Time and frequency features extracted from the postprocessed rPPG signal after applying the CHROM algorithm [5].

Domain	Feature	Description
Time	Zero crossing rate	Number of times the signal crossed the zero value
	Maximum/minimum	Quotient between the temporal maximum and minimum
Frequency	P	Maximum power response
	R	Quotient of P and the total power in the 0.6–4 Hz frequency range
	Mean	Mean value of the signal
	Spectral centroid	Mean value of each frequency component multiplied by its magnitude
	N_{max}/N	Sum of the N biggest values of the frequency signal divided by N
	LF Energy	Sum of the energy between 0 Hz and 4 Hz
	HF Energy	Sum of the energy between 2 Hz and 4 Hz

3.3   Classification

The last block of the presentation attack detection system is the classifier. Like in our reference work [11] we use Support Vector Machines (SVMs) as classifiers, in the present case considering the 9-dimensional features from Table 1 as input, and two classes as output: genuine face or face attack. Similar to related works [8], we use the signed distance to the separating surface obtained in the SVM training as output score of the Classifier in Fig. 2.

3.4   Integration of Individual Scores

In our experimental study we compare 4 different methods for the final stage in Fig. 2. The target of this stage is detecting the attacks as quick as possible (low Average Detection Delay, ADD), but trying to maintain a low value of real faces incorrectly detected as attacks (low False Non-Match Rate, FNMR). A deeper explanation of these terms can be found in [16].

Single Score. The first alternative only uses one input score for generating the fused PAD score (i.e., $N = 1$).

Mean Score. Individual PAD scores are averaged (applicable for $N > 1$).

Confidence-Based Combination. A weighted sum of input scores is applied. The **first way** explored to define the weights consists in a time decay function. This function considers older samples as less reliable than the newer ones, since as time passes the conditions are high likely to have changed. The more recent scores will have a bigger weight. The **second way** is based in a rPPG quality measure [2]. In this work we decided to calculate a SNR value from each rPPG signal. In order to do that, we consider a perfect rPPG signal as sinusoidal, and all the other frequencies different to the one most relevant are considered as noise. The scores with a higher SNR will have a bigger weight when computing the sum.

Quickest Change Detection. QCD is a statistical method that first estimates match and non-match distributions of the scores, and then tries to detect the moment in which the new scores change from one distribution to the other. This type of approach needs prior data in order to build the match and non-match distributions. Some variants of QCD also require to know the probability of intrusion in advance, so we decided to implement the MiniMax QCD (MQCD) algorithm from [16], which only needs the score distributions.

4   Databases and Experimental Protocol

4.1   Databases

We use two different databases in order to compare results. The first is a public dataset named 3D Mask Attack Database (3DMAD) from the Idiap Research Institute [6]. We decided to use 3DMAD to enable direct comparison with related studies, primarily with our reference work [11]. The second database is a self-collected dataset named BiDA HR (BiDA Heart Rate database). It has been captured with the goal of complementing existing databases like 3DMAD, which have several limitations such as low resolution, few spectrum bands and short duration.

The 3D Mask Attack Database (3DMAD) [6] contains frontal-view recordings of 17 different users acquired using Microsoft Kinect. The dataset is composed by 3 different sessions, two with genuine accesses and one with 3D mask presentation attacks. Each session contains 5 videos of 10 s, captured at 30 frames per second, with a resolution of 640×480 pixels. The length of the videos is one important limitation of this database, as it would be desirable to have longer video sequences in order to study continuous authentication and continuous PAD methods.

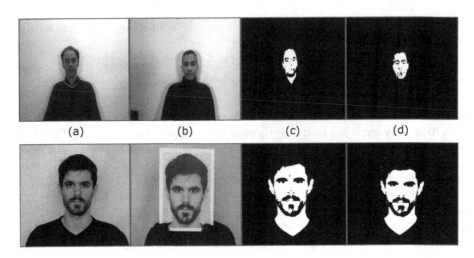

Fig. 3. Datasets: 3DMAD (top) and BiDA HR (bottom). From left to right: (a) genuine access attempt, (b) presentation attack. We also show the outputs from the skin detection algorithm in (c) and (d) from a genuine access and a presentation attack respectively.

The BiDA Heart Rate Database (BiDA HR) is a self collected dataset captured at the facilities of our research group at Universidad Autonoma de Madrid, in order to avoid the limitations from existent public databases. BiDA HR contains RGB, frontal-view, controlled, 60 s recordings of 10 different users, captured at 25 frames per second with 1920 × 1080 resolution (FullHD). It is a preliminary database and it has not been released yet. We are now capturing more samples to build a larger dataset. At its current state, the BiDA HR database is composed by 2 different sessions, one with real accesses and other with photo attacks. The artifacts of the attack attempts are HQ color printings of the faces (see Fig. 3). This way we are able to measure the performance of face PAD based on pulse detection with other type of easy-to-create spoofing artifacts different than 3D masks (the case in 3DMAD).

4.2   Experimental Protocol

From each rPPG signal we extracted the 9-dimensional feature vector described in Table 1. For classification in Fig. 2 we used Support Vector Machines with linear kernels and Cost parameter $C = 1000$ similarly to [11,12].

Two experiments are conducted: first we emulate the results in our previous work [11]. This experiment does not try to show the performance of continuous authentication but it tries to compare the performances of both core rPPG algorithms. The second experiment consists in obtaining performance measures when using the proposed methods for continuous PAD presented in Sect. 3.4.

The experimental protocol is the same for both databases (3DMAD and BiDA HR). First of all, the whole dataset is divided into genuine samples and presentation attack samples. Then, for the first experiment, in order to train and test the classifier, we use a Leave-One-Out Cross-Validation (LOOCV) protocol: for each subject in the database, we use all his feature vectors for testing a SVM model that has been trained with all the samples from the remaining users. The metric used to report results is the Equal Error Rate (EER in %). EER refers to the value where the Impostor Attack Presentation Match Rate (IAPMR, percentage of presentation attacks classified as real) and the False Non-Match Rate (FNMR, percentage of real faces classified as fake) are equal[1].

Results are obtained for several temporal window sizes: from 1 to 10 s in the case of 3DMAD, and also for 20, 40 and 60 s in the case of BiDA HR. For each temporal size T of the video segments, and considering a single video segment (i.e., $N = 1$ in Fig. 2), the EER has been calculated independently for all the subjects (each one of the LOOCV iterations). The individual results are then averaged to produce a single performance (mean and standard deviation of EER).

For the case of the continuous PAD experiments, we consider $N > 1$ in Fig. 2. In this case a PAD decision will be generated with a Delay of $D = N \times T$ seconds (video segments are not overlapped in time in our experiments).

Additionally, the QCD algorithm also needs prior data in order to build the match and non-match distributions. To compute those models, we use all data from 2 random users in each LOOCV iteration, who are left out of the LOOCV training and testing. In this case, additionally to the average EER rate, we have also computed an ADD-FNMR curve for varying temporal windows D. This curve is useful for showing the balance between the security and the usability of the continuous PAD approach proposed in Fig. 1.

Finally, for a deeper understanding of the QCD performance, we have also included some examples of the evolution of the fused PAD score during an example attack attempt. As the databases do not contain videos combining real faces and attacks, we have built videos concatenating a real access and an attack of the same user.

5   Results

5.1   Comparison with Reference Work

Table 2 shows the results of the comparison between the reference rPPG pipeline from [11] and the current work. Highlighted in bold are the best EER results for each value of the video length T. As can be seen in the table, none of the systems is absolutely better than the other in terms of performance. In general, the present system achieves lower EER rates than [11] when working with larger

---

[1] As error measures we have mentioned IAPMR and FNMR as defined and discussed by Galbally *et al.* [9]. Modifying the Decision Threshold until those error rates are equal we obtain the Presentation Attack Equal Error Rate, PAEER, defined and discussed in [9]. Here we follow [9] using PAEER to evaluate the presentation attacks, but calling it as EER for simplicity.

values of T (>5 s), but the differences in the error rates are low. If the databases contained less controlled conditions: more head motion, light changes, blur, etc., then we would expect more benefits from the skin detection and the CHROM algorithm proposed now, as they have shown to perform more robustly than [11] under these type of conditions.

Table 2. Comparison between the proposed rPPG face PAD and [11] on 3DMAD and BiDA HR databases. The study has been performed changing the length T of the video sequences analyzed. Values in %. Lower values for each window length T are highlighted in bold.

3DMAD	Length T [s]	1	2	3	4	5	6	7	8	9	10
[11]	Mean EER [%]	**42.8**	45.0	37.8	**40.7**	**33.1**	29.7	**25**	26.1	24.1	22.1
	Std EER [%]	5.0	5.9	8.6	9.8	10.8	18.1	14.5	15.2	11.9	10.3
Present Work	Mean EER [%]	44.7	**42.2**	**37.3**	46.1	46.1	**28.8**	26.1	**25.8**	**22.3**	**18.8**
	Std EER [%]	4.1	6.7	8.5	5.9	5.45	11.8	13.1	12.2	12.3	13.4

BiDA HR	Length T [s]	1	2	5	10	20	30	40	50	60
[11]	Mean EER [%]	**46.9**	**45.7**	**42.1**	40.1	40.0	40.0	36.6	**30.0**	**25.0**
	Std EER [%]	3.9	5.1	9.5	9.6	14.0	21.1	20.5	25.8	26.3
Present work	Mean EER [%]	48.5	46.5	43.1	**38.6**	**38.9**	**31.2**	**30.8**	32.5	26.2
	Std EER [%]	2.4	2.7	6.3	11.3	10.1	15.6	18.4	22.9	23.1

Comparing the EER results obtained with 3DMAD data with those obtained with BiDA HR, there is a gap between performances, achieving lower rates in the case of 3DMAD. As we discussed in [11], this seems to be due to the lower frame rate of BiDA HR.

5.2   Continuous PAD

PAD Score Integration. Figure 4 shows the PAD mean score combination from Sect. 3.4 on both databases. In that figure, the x axis corresponds to the values of $D = N \times T$, the delay for releasing the PAD decision (see Fig. 2), while the different curves represent the performances obtained with different temporal resolution T. It can be seen that, in general, the lowest EER (i.e., best PAD performance) is not obtained when using large T, but intermediate values (e.g. $T = 3$ s). With even shorter values of T (1 s or 2 s) the amount of available scores within each decision window will be higher, but the reliability of each individual score will be lower (as can be seen in Table 2). On the other hand, the individual scores obtained with large values of T are the most reliable, but in this case there will be little data to combine within each decision window of size D.

The reader can notice that the EER obtained for specific D and T may be higher than the results showed in Table 2 for equivalent values (note that T in Table 2 should be compared to D in Fig. 4). For example, this is the case of

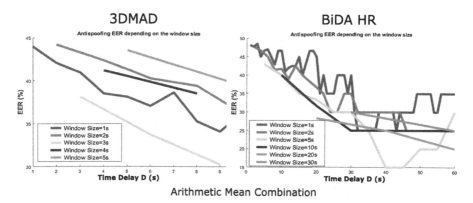

Fig. 4. Mean score combination of individual PAD scores, generated in temporal windows of varying duration on 3DMAD (left) and BiDA HR (right) databases. The x axis corresponds to the value of $D = N \times T$, the decision delay, while the different curves represent the performances obtained with different sizes of the temporal resolution T, and N is the number of individual PAD scores being combined.

$T = 1$ and $D = 10$ in Fig. 4 vs $T = 10$ in Table 2. While the classic approach (without the continuous loop in Fig. 1) is able to achieve a EER value of 18.8% at the 3DMAD database, the continuous PAD is only able of getting around 35%. However, the proposed continuous approach provides higher temporal resolution (decisions each second) and it is also able to improve the ongoing decisions by considering both old data and new one. The classic approach is only able to give one decision and only after the full 10 s have passed (high latency).

The best results from the 3 heuristic PAD methods compared (mean score, time based combination, and SNR-based combination) are obtained with the arithmetic mean. The SNR-based combination has failed to distinguish the samples with more quality from each recording. We think that modeling the pulse signal as a sinusoidal is not capturing appropriately the nature of a high quality pulse signal. With more accurate models it might be possible to achieve lower error rates using this approach. Finally, the temporal confidence fails to achieve lower EER rates than the other methods, and we think this is mainly caused by the limitations of the employed databases. This confidence measure is designed to deal with variable scenarios in which the conditions (attack/non attack) change within the same video. However these databases only contain recordings of attacks and real attempts performed separately. If this method was applied to a more realistic scenario, the results might be better than the ones obtained with the other two heuristic methods.

Quickest Change Detection (QCD). Figure 5 shows the ADD-FNMR curves obtained with the QCD algorithm for the 3DMAD and BiDA HR databases. The different pairs of values of ADD and FNMR have been computed varying the decision threshold for each temporal segment T. The results from both databases show the same properties. In these curves, the best choice of ADD-

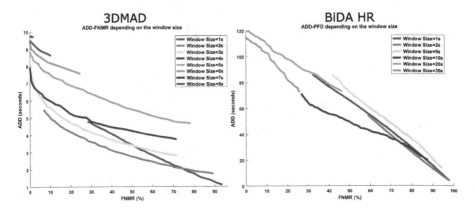

Fig. 5. Average Presentation Attack Detection Delay (ADD) vs False Non-Match Rate (FNMR) obtained on the 3DMAD (left) and BiDA HR (right) databases, for different temporal segments T.

FNMR depends of the real application of the system. Generally, a lower area under the curve is an indicator of a better performance. As can be seen in Fig. 4, the best results (as a balance of usability and security) are obtained with medium values of T, as it provides a good balance between the reliability of the scores and a low latency. When working with large values of T it is impossible to achieve low ADDs because of the inherent latency due to the analyzed temporal segments, of duration T. This limitation does not exist when working with small T, but these approaches are unable to obtain FNMR values as low as the obtained with a bigger T, due to the smaller reliability of the individual PAD scores being fused.

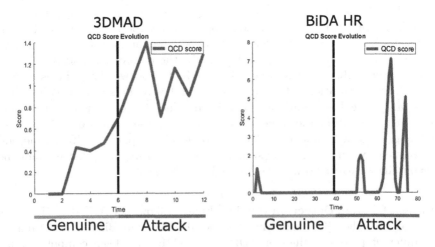

Fig. 6. Temporal evolution of the fused PAD scores (QCD) in a variable attack scenario. The attacker puts on the mask inside the example video. Results using data from 3DMAD (left) and BiDA HR (right) are shown.

Finally, Fig. 6 shows an example of the evolution of the liveness scores obtained with the MQCD algorithm. In this scenario we wanted to simulate a real situation in which the attacker puts on the mask inside the video, so we have concatenated two different videos from the same user (a real access and an attack attempt). The higher the scores the higher the estimated probability of a presentation attack. Thanks to the MQCD and its low latency approach, the PAD score is able to evolve over the video, and can be compared to a threshold to detect the intrusion with low latency.

6   Conclusions and Future Work

In this paper, we have studied face Presentation Attack Detection (PAD) based on remote PhothoPlethysmoGraphy (rPPG) or, in other words, video-based heart rate estimation. We have extracted pulse information from facial videos from two different databases: 3DMAD and BiDA HR. These databases contain videos with different resolutions, frame rates, durations, and spoofing artifacts.

We have compared the performance of a new rPPG system based on a combination of a skin detector and a chrominance method, and the system used in our previous work [11], which was based on Blind Source Separation techniques. Even though the chrominance-based system is more robust to variable light conditions, blur, and other factors, in this work both systems perform in a similar way due to the controlled conditions found in 3DMAD and BiDA HR.

We have also analyzed several approaches for low-latency continuous PAD. The first approach combines individual PAD scores with simple rules obtained from consecutive small video segments. The arithmetic mean of consecutive scores outperforms SNR-based and temporal-based score combination functions. The second approximation to continuous PAD uses a Quickest Change Detection algorithm (MQCD) for getting a balance between low attack detection delays (ADD) and low false positive rates (FNMR). Best results were obtained by generating individual PAD scores from video segments of around 3 s. We also discussed a possible time-variant attack scenario in which the attacker puts on the mask in the middle of the video. In this scenario, the advantages of a short-time rPPG analysis can be fully exploited.

Future work includes: (1) Improving the baseline system for getting lower EER with short videos (e.g. using video magnification techniques [3]). (2) Capturing a larger database with a higher number of users, more variate spoofing artifacts, and also more challenging conditions (like ambient illumination, blur, occlusions, etc.). (3) Accomplishing a more in depth study of the performance when changing spatial and temporal resolution of videos. And (4) developing more robust quality metrics in rPPG [2] for score combination in continuous PAD and continuous authentication [8].

Acknowledgements. This work was supported in part by Accenture, project Cogni-Metrics from MINECO/FEDER under Grant TEC2015-70627-R, and project Neuro-metrics (CEALAL/2017-13) from UAM-Banco Santander. The work of J. Hernandez-Ortega was supported by a Ph.D. Scholarship from Universidad Autonoma de Madrid.

References

1. Allen, J.: Photoplethysmography and its application in clinical physiological measurement. Physiol. Measur. **28**(3), R1–R39 (2007)
2. Alonso-Fernandez, F., Fierrez, J., Ortega-Garcia, J.: Quality measures in biometric systems. IEEE Secur. Priv. **10**(6), 52–62 (2012)
3. Bharadwaj, S., Dhamecha, T.I., Vatsa, M., Singh, R.: Computationally efficient face spoofing detection with motion magnification. In: IEEE Conference on Computer Vision and Pattern Recognition Workshops (CVPRW), pp. 105–110 (2013)
4. Dargie, W.: Analysis of time and frequency domain features of accelerometer measurements. In: International Conference on Computer Communication and Networks. IEEE (2009)
5. De Haan, G., Jeanne, V.: Robust pulse rate from chrominance-based rPPG. IEEE Trans. Biomed. Eng. **60**(10), 2878–2886 (2013)
6. Erdogmus, N., Marcel, S.: Spoofing face recognition with 3D masks. IEEE Trans. Inf. Forensics Secur. **9**(7), 1084–1097 (2014)
7. Fierrez, J., Pozo, A., Martinez-Diaz, M., Galbally, J., Morales, A.: Benchmarking touchscreen biometrics for mobile authentication. IEEE Trans. Inf. Forensics Secur. **13**(11), 2720–2733 (2018)
8. Fierrez, J., Morales, A., Vera-Rodriguez, R., Camacho, D.: Multiple classifiers in biometrics. Part 2: trends and challenges. Inf. Fusion **44**, 103–112 (2018)
9. Galbally, J., Gomez-Barrero, M., Ross, A.: Accuracy evaluation of handwritten signature verification: rethinking the random-skilled forgeries dichotomy. In: IEEE International Joint Conference on Biometrics (IJCB), pp. 302–310 (2017)
10. Hadid, A., Evans, N., Marcel, S., Fierrez, J.: Biometrics systems under spoofing attack: an evaluation methodology and lessons learned. IEEE Sig. Process. Mag. **32**(5), 20–30 (2015)
11. Hernandez-Ortega, J., Fierrez, J., Morales, A., Tome, P.: Time analysis of pulse-based face anti-spoofing in visible and NIR. In: IEEE CVPR Computer Society Workshop on Biometrics (2018)
12. Li, X., Komulainen, J., Zhao, G., Yuen, P.C., Pietikäinen, M.: Generalized face anti-spoofing by detecting pulse from face videos. In: International Conference on Pattern Recognition (ICPR), pp. 4244–4249. IEEE (2016)
13. Mahmoud, T.M., et al.: A new fast skin color detection technique. World Acad. Sci. Eng. Technol. **43**, 501–505 (2008)
14. Marcel, S., Nixon, M.S., Fierrez, J., Evans, N.: Handbook of Biometric Anti-Spoofing, 2nd edn. Springer, Heidelberg (2019)
15. McDuff, D., Gontarek, S., Picard, R.W.: Improvements in remote cardiopulmonary measurement using a five band digital camera. IEEE Trans. Biomed. Eng. **61**(10), 2593–2601 (2014)
16. Perera, P., Patel, V.M.: Efficient and low latency detection of intruders in mobile active authentication. IEEE Trans. Inf. Forensics Secur. **13**(6), 1392–1405 (2018)
17. Poh, M.Z., McDuff, D.J., Picard, R.W.: Advancements in noncontact, multiparameter physiological measurements using a webcam. IEEE Trans. Biomed. Eng. **58**(1), 7–11 (2011)
18. Rapczynski, M., Werner, P., Al-Hamadi, A.: Continuous low latency heart rate estimation from painful faces in real time. In: International Conference on Pattern Recognition (ICPR), pp. 1165–1170 (2016)
19. Tasli, H.E., Gudi, A., den Uyl, M.: Remote PPG based vital sign measurement using adaptive facial regions. In: Proceedings of IEEE International Conference on Image Processing (ICIP), pp. 1410–1414 (2014)

Author Index

Printed in the United States
By Bookmasters